Walking with God in the Quiet Places

Kay Arthur • Emilie Barnes
Julie Clinton • Elizabeth George
Sharon Jaynes • Stormie Omartian
Jennifer Rothschild • Lysa TerKeurst

HARVEST HOUSE PUBLISHERS

EUGENE, OREGON

Cover by Garborg Design Works, Savage, Minnesota

WALKING WITH GOD IN THE QUIET PLACES

Copyright © 2009 by Harvest House Publishers
Published by Harvest House Publishers
Eugene, Oregon 97402
www.harvesthousepublishers.com

ISBN 978-0-7369-2798-7

Printed in China

09 10 11 12 13 14 15 16 17 / RDS-NI / 10 9 8 7 6 5 4 3 2 1

Contents

Kay Arthur

Emilie Barnes

The fruit of righteousness will be peace;
the effect of righteousness will be
quietness and confidence forever.

ISAIAH 32:17 NIV

But as for me, how good it is to be near God!
I have made the Sovereign Lord my shelter,
and I will tell everyone
about the wonderful things you do.

PSALM 73:28 NLT

Worth a Thousand Words

*S*ometimes I like to read the Gospels as if I'm thumbing through a photo album chock-full of snapshots, glancing at each one. Recently, in Matthew 9, a great snapshot of Jesus reclining at a dinner party caught my eye.

It's a picture of Jesus and His disciples sharing a meal at Matthew's house—along with an apparently motley crew of sinners. The Pharisees in attendance that day with them were irritated and befuddled by how someone who claimed to be a rabbi could lower Himself and have dinner with such riffraff.

The smug Pharisees asked Jesus' disciples about it. (And can't you just hear the contemptuous sniff?) "Why does your teacher eat with tax collectors and 'sinners'?"

Before His disciples could formulate their thoughts and answer the Pharisees, Jesus Himself spoke up. "It is not the healthy who need a doctor, but the sick" (Matthew 9:12 NIV).

Did you catch that? The Word specifically says that Jesus answered the question of the Pharisees even though it was asked of the disciples.

Now, why did Jesus answer a question that was clearly not directed to Him? The query was obviously aimed at Peter,

John, and the boys. Maybe it's because the question directly related to Jesus and not to His followers.

Think about that for a moment. Keep your eye on that picture of Jesus and His disciples. Do you think the disciples that were gathered at Matthew's home that day could have answered the question well? If you were there, could you have answered well? Most likely they could have. And most likely you, too, could have come up with a reasonable defense for why Jesus chose to dine with society's lesser lights. But neither we nor His disciples could have answered as well as Jesus did!

This shows me that some questions are better left for Christ Himself, even if the questioner happens to direct the query at you or me. So here's a novel way of looking at it: Perhaps the questions that most directly relate to Christ should be left for Christ to answer for Himself.

People will ask questions like "Why do the innocent suffer?" Or maybe "Why does God allow evil?" The fact is, I really don't have a lot of zingy answers when I am confronted with those kinds of questions. As His disciple, I have an idea, but I don't hold the definitive answers. Only God does.

To assume ownership of the mysteries of God, as if I truly understand and can explain them, would be an arrogant, ignorant thing to do, and it wouldn't help the honest questioner at all. On the other hand, to pause after a question is asked (instead of barging in and blurting out a pithy religious answer) gives the Master Teacher an opportunity to overhear and answer for Himself, just as He did that day in Matthew's home.

We all must practice a spiritual conversation that has enough pauses for Jesus to interrupt. The discourse of our lives is full of unanswerable questions.

Let Jesus interrupt and show who He is, not just who you *think* He is. Our answers offer a limited view of Him. To confine the infinite in finite terms is silly. To attempt explaining omniscience with our limited breadth of understanding is equally unhelpful. God is capable of defending His position when He so chooses. He is unruffled by scrutiny and undaunted by interrogation.

Let Him be God, and you can focus on being His follower. When you are asked a tough question about the one you serve, pause, look toward the Master, and listen for His voice. God is always listening, and He will always answer a sincere questioner. You and I, as His disciples, are often questioned, and we should be prepared to offer good answers. But don't let your good answer simply placate a questioner when Christ Himself could offer the best and most satisfying answer. He will reveal Himself to those who wish to see, and He will speak to those who want to hear.

And one glimpse, one picture of Christ, is worth a thousand of our words.

> *When you are brought before synagogues, rulers and authorities, do not worry about how you will defend yourselves or what you will say, for the Holy Spirit will teach you at that time what you should say* (Luke 12:11-12 NIV).

EMILIE BARNES

A Treasure in Jars of Clay

*But we have this treasure in jars of clay
to show that this all-surpassing power
is from God and not from us.*

2 CORINTHIANS 4:7 NIV

When our son, Brad, was in high school, he really enjoyed taking courses in ceramics. Even though I am his mother, I can say he was very good. In fact, many of his prized vases, jars, and pots still adorn our home. When I looked at a lump of reddish-tan clay, I was amazed that Brad was able to make a beautiful vessel out of it. When he added color and glaze, it became a masterpiece.

In today's scripture we read that we are "jars of clay." We have a great treasure in us, and this all-surpassing power is from God and not from us.

We live in a world that tells us that if we are righteous enough we can become little gods. However, our reading says that we (Christians) are jars of clay with this great treasure (Jesus Christ) in us. I can go to any nursery in our area and purchase an inexpensive clay pot. They're not of much value. On the other hand, my dictionary defines "treasure" as wealth or riches, something of great value. While we hide our treasures in vaults or safe-deposit boxes, God trusts His treasure in a common clay pot! The only value our clay pot has is in the treasure inside.

If we believe that this is true, then we will want to share that treasure inside of us with others. I am continually amazed how God can use me, just an ordinary person. We need to show others that this all-surpassing power is from God and not from us. Philippians 4:13 (NIV) states, "I can do everything through him who gives me strength."

Can you trust God today to believe that you, a clay pot with a great treasure inside, can do all things because Christ Jesus has given you the strength and power to do it? If we could believe this promise, we would change ourselves, our families, our churches, our cities, our country, and the world. Trust God today for this belief.

> *Father God, even though I am an inexpensive clay pot, You make me valuable because You live in me. Thank You for that gift. Amen.*

JULIE CLINTON

A Life of Influence

*In everything set them an example
by doing what is good.*

TITUS 2:7 NIV

You will influence other people today. What message will they get from you? Better yet, how will they describe you after today?

Whether we realize it or not, we influence other people's lives. Sometimes we intentionally choose to influence others, but other times we are completely unaware of our impact. The influence of both our good and our bad gestures and words is immeasurable. Perhaps God intended it that way to keep us humble. Often, the people we touch don't realize the effect we had until years later. But what matters most is that we are willing to make every day count by investing in the life of another human being. Make a plan to increase your influence in the lives you can realistically touch. Your investment in other people is the only thing that will outlast you.

You are the hands and feet of Christ, and others are influenced in their own walk with Him by watching you live out yours. To live in a way that lifts up Jesus and honors

God is a mighty big calling, but it's something we must do every day.

What message are you sending to the girl behind the counter at the supermarket? To your children? To your coworkers? The question isn't whether you are making a difference. That's a given. The question is, what kind of difference are you making?

> *Use my life, Lord, as an example of Your love. Use my hands to show kindness. Use my tongue to speak praise. Use my mouth to spread joy and laughter. Let all that I am help others to experience Your love. Amen.*

Setting Priorities

But seek first his kingdom and his righteousness,
and all these things will be given to you as well.

Matthew 6:33 niv

What if you were given $86,400 every day for the rest of your life? What would you do with it? Let's add one caveat. You have to spend all of it each day! Could you do it? How would you spend it? Tough decision, right? Guess what—God gives you 86,400 seconds every day, and you spend every one! Every day! How are you using your time?

Most of us are so harried and desperate just to get through another day that we don't take the time to step back and ask ourselves if what we're doing really matters and if our activities reflect our priorities. Often the two are disconnected, though we may be too busy to see it. But the Bible says, "For where your treasure is, there your heart will be also" (Matthew 6:21 niv).

Do the things you do reflect eternal treasures? Are you seeking His kingdom with the time you've been given? What are you pouring your heart into? Take a personal inventory. Find out where you're investing your time, and whether the expenditure reflects your priorities. Be sure to spend your time wisely. You never get it back!

> *Dear Lord, You have given me every minute of the day as a precious gift. Help me to use my time wisely on the things that are most important to You and to me. Let me see clearly what You want me to do with my time, and give me the courage to say no to those things that just clutter my day. Amen.*

Expecting a Call

God has a great purpose for each one of us. There is a call from God on your life and mine. The question is, will we listen to find out what it is?

We can be in the dark about the call of God on our lives for two reasons: either we have not heard God's call and we're living as though we have, or we have heard God's call and we're living as though we have not.

I've seen many people who were too busy, too drugged out, too tired, too preoccupied, or too in pursuit of riches and fame to hear God calling them. Others were afraid they might be called to insignificance, so they didn't want to know about it. I've known others still who clearly heard the call of God and ran away from it. They refused to take the call. I've also known people with such a low opinion of themselves that they didn't believe God had them destined for anything great. So when the call came, they thought it must be for somebody else and didn't respond.

It never entered my mind that I had a life's calling until I was in my early thirties, and then I thought about it with deep regret. I was certain that by this late in life, I had passed up any opportunities for God to do something significant through me. Having lived far away from Him for so long, I despaired over what I considered an unredeemable loss. It wasn't until I understood that God is a Redeemer who redeems *all* things—even our past—that I began to have hope. The Bible says that "the gifts and the calling of God are irrevocable" (Romans 11:29 NASB). When God issues a call, He doesn't take it back. He only waits for us to move into it.

Many people know their calling but can't see how it will ever be realized in the details of their lives. That's because they are trying to accomplish it in their own strength. But God doesn't say, "Here's what I want you to do with your life, now go do it." He first gives a vision and then says, "Walk step by step with Me and *I'll* do it through you."

The only reason it appears that some people are "more called" by God than others is that they were expecting the call and answered it.

Prayer Light

Lord, I know You have great purpose for me and a plan for my life. Open my ears to hear Your voice leading me into all You have for me. Align my heart with Yours and prepare me to understand where You would have me to go and what You would have me to do. Help me to hear Your call. If my expectations and plans are out of alignment with Your will for me, I surrender them to You. I don't want to be unfruitful and unfulfilled because I never clearly heard Your call. I want You to fill me with Your greatness so that I may do great things for others as You have called me to do. I commit to walking this road step-by-step with You so that I may fully become all that You have made me to be.

> *The God of our Lord Jesus Christ, the Father of glory, may give to you the spirit of wisdom and revelation in the knowledge of Him, the eyes of your understanding being enlightened; that you may know what is the hope of His calling, what are the riches of the glory of His inheritance in the saints, and what is the exceeding greatness of His power toward us who believe, according to the working of His mighty power.*
>
> Ephesians 1:17-19 nkjv

Mining for Gold

When he has tested me,
I will come forth as gold.

JOB 23:10 NIV

❧

knelt beside the creek bed, surrounded by 30 fourth graders panning for gold. We were at Reid Gold Mine, and I was the chaperone of the rowdy young miners. The tour guide took us through dark, musty tunnels, explaining how the miners a hundred years ago searched for veins of gold embedded in the rocks and hidden beneath the sodden walls. Many tirelessly panned for gold in the mountain stream in hopes of finding a few valuable nuggets.

After the tour, we each grabbed a sieve and tried our luck. First we lowered pans into the mud of the streambed and filled our sieves. Then we shook the sieves back and forth, allowing the crystal clear water to flow over its contents. The silt filtered through the screen and fell back into the stream as hopeful children (and a few adults) searched for gold. Unfortunately none of us struck it rich that day, but I did discover a valuable treasure.

As I filled my sieve with mud, I saw a reflection of my life filled with filth and pain. Then, as I shook the bowl back and forth, the cool, pure water of God's Spirit washed over me. I imagined God washing through my memories and the dirt falling to the ground, leaving nuggets of gold behind.

Our lives, no matter how messy, are filled with gold nuggets. We need to look beyond the dirt and allow God to expose the treasures just waiting to be discovered.

Words of Faith When Pressures Build

*A*re you living life in overdrive? Do you ever feel like running away, checking out, giving up?

Life is filled with pressure, pressure, pressure.

Pressure to be. Pressure to do. Pressure to perform. Pressure to produce.

And with the pressures come anxiety and stress, especially to the Christian who longs to be pleasing to God.

Am I being the mate I should be? The parent I should be? Am I handling everything the way I ought to as His child?

Life is so accelerated. Hurrying to work. Dashing to get the kids to their activities. Hurrying to prepare meals. Rushing to get to church.

You think you're going to slow down when the kids get back to school…come winter…come Christmas…come summer…come vacation.

But it doesn't happen. Realistically, life is never going to slow down; the pressure is never going to lessen; the stress will always be there in one form or another. So what are you going to do about it? Tough it out until you break? Run into some ungodly escape hatch? Give up? Check out?

The good news is: You don't have to choose any of the above. God knows about the pressure, the stress, the anxiety, the accelerated pace of our earthly life, and He has provided a "way of escape…so that you will be able to endure it" (1 Corinthians 10:13 NASB).

It's all wrapped up in our communion with God, what I call "going into the sanctuary." And there is one element of communion with God that I believe is a vital key to releasing pressure or stress. That key is worship through music: praising God in song.

During Paul's second missionary journey, the apostle and his compatriot Silas found their ministry causing a riot, and they felt the brunt of it. Their clothes were torn from them, and they were beaten and thrown into prison.

Stress? Yes!

Anxiety? Every legitimate reason for it!

How did Paul and Silas handle it? What kept them from breaking?

Acts 16:25 (NASB) gives us the answer: "But about midnight Paul and Silas were praying and singing hymns of praise to God." They turned their focus from the present pressures of their lives to the throne of their sovereign Abba Father—and the tension was relieved.

When sheep become tense, edgy, and restless, the shepherd will quietly move through the flock, and his very presence will release the tension of the sheep and quiet their anxieties. Their shepherd is there!

And this is what happens when we begin to worship our Lord and our God in song. We move into a consciousness of His presence, and the tension begins to unravel, the tautness of the pressure eases, anxieties become meaningless, for we are reminded that He is there—our Jehovah Shammah, our all-sufficient, sovereign God. He inhabits the praises of His people (Psalm 22:3).

The more you enter into His courts with praise and into His gates with thanksgiving, the less you will feel the stress, the pressure, the anxiety of daily life, for you will have...

> *set your mind on the things above, not on the things that are on earth. For you have died and your life is hidden with Christ in God* (Colossians 3:2-3 NASB).

Spiritual Insights

*I also, after I heard of your faith in
the Lord Jesus and your love for all the saints,
do not cease to give thanks for you,
making mention of you in my prayers.*

EPHESIANS 1:15 NKJV

When we love people, we can't help but pray for them because we carry them in our hearts. And when friends are far away and we're unable to express our love and support personally, we can pray knowing that God hears us. Jesus prayed for His disciples. Paul prayed for the believers in Philippi, the Christians in Colossae, and for his friends in Ephesus. When it comes to your friends and friendships, there are many reasons to turn to God in prayer! What can you do?

Praise God for your friends. You've been blessed with special people in your life. Give thanks for them.

Pray for their spiritual well-being and insights. Paul prayed for believers to have their spiritual eyes opened so they would recognize their spiritual blessings.

Pray for the body of Christ, the church. Pray for your friends to make Jesus the Lord and Savior of their lives. And give thanks for Christ and His leadership.

Every prayer you lift up for your friends and for others who are placed on your heart reaches God's ears and heart. Ask Him to use His power, might, strength, and wisdom to help the people you care about.

From God's Word to Your Heart

Paul was a prisoner when he wrote with such conviction about compassionate prayer for others. You would expect an innocent prisoner to rant, rave, blame others, question God, and sink into depression. But not Paul. He praised God! His outbursts of worship and lists of blessings run through his entire letter to the believers in Philippi. The overflow of Paul's heart is evidence that he meditated on God's sovereign plan, the Holy Spirit's indwelling, Jesus' supremacy, and the shining effects of God's grace.

Pray as Paul did! No matter your circumstances or your troubles, ask God to help you and the people in your life develop "spiritual eyes" for seeing and understanding your riches and blessings in Jesus Christ. Tell Him you want to...

- know Him better
- look with great hope and anticipation to His upward calling
- understand your special relationship as His child and heir

- experience His power moment by moment in
  your life

What are your difficult circumstances today? You might be limited by a life situation, but God is never hampered. Praise Him!

Why not write a few words of hope and comfort to a loved one who needs encouragement? Or call someone who needs God's peace and pray with him or her. And share spiritual insights from God's Word.

> *Lord, thank You for hearing my prayers for my friends. For those who don't know You, help me be an example of Your love and grace. And for those friends who know You, I pray they will see Your hand in their lives. May we all give You glory. Amen.*

Don't Send Me to Africa

*The eyes of the Lord range throughout
the earth to strengthen those whose
hearts are fully committed to him.*

2 CHRONICLES 16:9 NIV

❧

Since I was a little girl I've had a heart for the people of Africa. To be honest, though, I didn't want to be a missionary who lived in a hut, ate grubs fried on an open flame, and wore tribal headdresses. What a limited view of Africa I had. So while I prayed for the people of Africa, I would always throw in, "But, Lord, don't send me." I can just imagine God smiling and looking back at me saying, "Really, princess? You don't want to go to Africa…fine. Then I'll send Africa to you."

And that's exactly what He did. One night while attending a concert by the Liberian Boys Choir, God clearly spoke to my heart and told me that two of those boys were mine. I tried to ignore Him, but to no avail. At the end of the concert, two of the boys walked straight up to me, wrapped their arms around me, and called me Mom. After months of prayer and piles of paperwork, we went to pick up our two sons, Mark and Jackson. Africa had come to our home.

No longer was the plight of the starving orphans in Africa a nameless face on TV; they were precious children who deserved a second chance. Not only did we think so, but other people in my church soon felt moved to also adopt children from Liberia. Today, as I walk up to church on Sunday mornings, I am always moved by the precious sight I see. A little white hand holding a little black hand, a brother and sister skipping and laughing together! And something in my heart just knows this is the way it's supposed to be.

This is the way the body of Christ is supposed to work. God speaks, we listen; He confirms, we obey; He gives us the strength to do amazing things, we watch miracles come out of our lives. I love 2 Chronicles 16:9 because it brings a picture to my mind of God standing in front of a crowd of people asking, "Who is willing to do an amazing assignment for Me?"

Many shrug and make excuses. But one little girl jumps up and in complete abandon says, "Me, Lord! Me! Pick me! I am willing!" Then God smiles, scoops her up, brings her into His loving embrace, and whispers back, "Well done, My child. I am so pleased. You have made the good choice. I will give you the strength to do this. Do not be afraid. I will be with you."

Dear Lord, let me always be that little girl with the up-stretched arm and obedient heart. Give me the wisdom to know Your voice and the courage to say yes to whatever You ask of me. My greatest desire is to walk with You all the days of my life. I don't want to settle for the good life. I want the great life, where I live the adventure You created my soul to live. In Jesus' name. Amen.

JULIE CLINTON

Everyday Graces

*From the fullness of his grace we have all
received one blessing after another.*

JOHN 1:16 NIV

Most of the time when we talk about God's grace, we are referring to the gift of salvation. But God's grace also comes in tiny little packages marked "A Gift for You." Each day God presents gifts of His grace. Most of the time we take them for granted.

Take some time to appreciate some of these gifts:

- freedom to be real
- quiet moments
- the brilliant colors of spring
- walking
- knowing you're loved
- a friend who listens
- a child's hug

Start looking at each of these as little dreams come true. God's dream for us unfolds in thousands of little ways through everyday graces He places in our lives.

Too often we are just too busy to notice. Or we are so eager to have the big dream come true, we forget to watch for little things that *are* the dream coming true.

Most Christians can trust God for heaven and eternity with Him, but we struggle to trust Him for everyday life. Start seeing and living differently—it will turn your life around!

> *Thank You, God, for Your abounding grace, for the tremendous gift of salvation, and for the thousands of little graces You send my way each day. Amen.*

The Hidden Strength of Pain

> *I take limitations in stride, and with good cheer, these limitations that cut me down to size—abuse, accidents, opposition, bad breaks. I just let Christ take over! And so the weaker I get, the stronger I become.*
>
> 2 CORINTHIANS 12:10 MSG

God is not wasting the pain in your life. He never wastes a wound. He's healing you at this very moment and using that pain to show you a dream bigger than you realize. But you need to trust Him. When you trust, you allow room for hope.

When we are in the deep, deep valley, we must hold on to the assurance that God stands firm and strong behind us. Nothing we experience will be wasted. It will all be used for our good—to make us stronger, to make us walk closer to Him, to give us a more loving heart. In our greatest pain we need to lean heavily on God. He's using our weakness to do His work in and through us, building trust, so that His dream for each of our lives can become a reality.

We rarely understand how God is using pain in our lives to

refine us. Sometimes through the tears we can't see anything, much less understand. But just because we don't understand the pain doesn't mean He's not using it. He is. It's part of His plan and purpose. Trust Him.

> *Dear God, some days I don't know how I will get through the day with the pain and hurt I have to face. Let me feel Your presence, Lord, so I can trust You and relax. Let me fall into Your everlasting arms, giving You control as I feel Your strength. Amen.*

Living a Timothy Lifestyle

*I trust in the Lord Jesus to send Timothy to
you shortly, that I also may be encouraged
when I know your state. For I have no one
like-minded, who will sincerely care for your
state. For all seek their own, not the things
which are of Christ Jesus. But you know
his proven character, that as a son with his
father he served with me in the gospel.*

PHILIPPIANS 2:19-22 NKJV

Have you ever said "Yes, but…"? It's amazing how
one tiny word—*but*—can send such a strong signal
of lack of faith or understanding. Do you contemplate the
sacrifices made by Christ and think, "Yes, but that was *Jesus*!
That was God in the flesh. I'm 'just' human."

Consider that Jesus thought of others all the time, He
served people all the time (even when He was in prayer, it
was to be refreshed so He could help us), and He submitted
His will to His Father. Wouldn't it be great to be like that?
"Yes, but…"

Well, the apostle Paul knew that a few of us might respond

with that small but powerfully negative word. He introduces us to his assistant and traveling companion, Timothy, and says, "Okay, here's another person like me who thinks of others and not of himself." Timothy was "just" a human too. But he learned how to be a faithful servant. He grew that way because he was first a faithful student. May Timothy's example help you change your "Yes, but…" to a "Yes, and I will…" There are no valid excuses to keep you from being a servant of the Lord.

From God's Word to Your Heart

How can you become more like Paul and Timothy in your service to the Lord and to the people around you?

Submit to God. You are His servant.

Submit to another. Perhaps to become a Timothy you need to submit to a Paul. Do you have someone you serve with shoulder-to-shoulder? Is there an older woman or another woman you help as she serves the Lord?

Mature in usefulness. Sharpen your ministry skills and attitudes. Strengthen your faith. Increase your knowledge of the sacred Scriptures.

Be content to play second fiddle. Harmony is produced in ministry when everyone seeks to be a servant.

Commit to "The Four A's." Will you sign the statement below, which was presented at a conference I attended?

For You, Lord…

Anything
Anywhere
Any time
At any cost
Name_____Date_____

What one behavior, heart concern, loyalty, or sacrifice drawn from the example of Timothy can you weave into your life of humble service to God's people?

> *Lord, help me serve side-by-side with others to bring glory to Your name through compassion, teaching, and faithfulness. When I discount my potential as a servant because of my mistakes or lack of understanding, help me say yes to You and persevere. Amen.*

Buddy Breathing

*If one falls down,
his friend can help him up.*

ECCLESIASTES 4:10 NIV

⁂

*L*et's go scuba diving!" a friend exclaimed one hot summer day.

"That sounds great," I said. "But I don't know how."

"Just leave it to me," he said.

I was 17 the first time I went scuba diving. My friend strapped an oxygen tank on his back, a mask on his face, and flippers on his feet. I only had a mask and flippers.

"Where's my oxygen?" I asked.

"I've got it," he answered as he patted the tank on his back.

So into the ocean we plunged. He put his arm around my waist as if I were a sack of potatoes and down we went. John drew oxygen from the tank and then passed the breathing apparatus to me. We took turns breathing the oxygen in what he called "buddy breathing." It occurred to me that I was totally dependent on this young boy to keep me alive!

Throughout my life the words of friends have been like

oxygen when I felt as if I were drowning. God has sent people my way who have strapped on the Word of God and passed the life-giving words to me when I've needed them most.

Buddy breathing. That's what we can do for each other when a friend forgets how to draw in the air she needs. That's what God does for us each time we open His Word.

Refinished and Restored

*If anyone is in Christ, he is a new creation;
the old has gone, the new has come!*

2 CORINTHIANS 5:17 NIV

"Sharon, do you realize how much time and energy it's going to take to refinish that old table and chairs?" my mother asked as she perused my latest purchase.

When I was a teenager I had a fetish for antiques and old furniture and bought a number of pieces at auctions, flea markets, and estate sales. Often when I brought my treasures home, my family would roll their eyes and say, "I can't believe you paid money for that dirty piece of junk."

But I never saw my purchases as junk. They just needed a little work...okay, a lot of work. Thinking back, I believe my love for refinishing old, beat-up furniture had something to do with how I viewed my life and how God refinished me.

Like the old table, I was on the auctioning block, and God purchased me with Christ's blood. I had layers and layers of my old self that had to be stripped away to reveal the beauty hidden beneath. God sanded me with life experiences and trials to remove my rough edges. He glued my loose joints and mended my broken pieces. Then He put a sealer on me and in me—the Holy Spirit—who brought out the beauty of who God created me to be.

After I finished refurbishing the old table and chairs, I sat in the garage thinking about all God had done in my life. My mom opened the door, looked at the old table, and said, "Oh my. I never thought something so ugly could turn out so beautiful."

I said, "Amen."

Beginning to See the Light

Our lives are touched by many different kinds of light.

Sunlight and moonlight. Stoplights and spotlights. Firelight, city lights, candlelight, and lamplight. Headlights, night-lights, neon lights, and streetlights. Glittering and blinding lights. Confusing and deceiving lights.

All of these lights have one thing in common. They eventually go out. They're not reliable. They can never be the light we need to illuminate the path of our life. There is only one light that never goes out. It comes from God.

It *is* God.

God's light is the true light. His light makes clear. All other light confuses. His light *reveals* the truth. All other light obscures it. His light brings us out of our blindness and helps us see in a way we've never been able to see before. He says, "I will bring the blind by a way they did not know; I will lead them in paths they have not known. I will make darkness light before them, and crooked places straight. These things I will do for them, and not forsake them" (Isaiah

42:16 NKJV). God's light penetrates darkness, and darkness cannot put it out.

Unless we follow the true light, we are being led into darkness.

In the years before I had a personal relationship with God, I walked in a thick darkness of depression, fear, anxiety, and despair. Everything I experimented with was a desperate search for something to light up my life. But I never found anything lasting. When I received the Lord, I was not suddenly flooded with light, as some people have described it. The light I saw was a glimmer of hope. I compare it to sleeping in a dark room with a pinhole of light entering through the curtain and shining brightly in your eyes. It's a small light, but noticeably bright enough to awaken you if you've grown accustomed to the blackness of the room. The light of the Lord was that unmistakable to me because of the contrasting darkness of my life. Any more light would have been blinding. But because of my own bondage, the light was dim at the beginning of my walk compared to what was to come. The more I walked in the light of the Lord, the brighter it became, until it lit up every part of my being.

I have heard people talk about near-death experiences where they saw a bright light. I don't doubt that they saw it. But I know that when we who believe in the Lord die, we won't see *a* light. We will see *the* light. We will see Jesus who is the light of the world.

Prayer Light

Lord, You are the light of my life. You illuminate my path, and I will follow wherever You lead. Shield me from being lured by the light of the world. Keep me from being deceived by the light of evil. Protect me from being blinded by the light that confuses. Help me to always identify the counterfeit. I depend on You to lift up the light of Your countenance upon me (Psalm 4:6). Thank You, Lord, that because You never change, Your light is constant in my life no matter what is going on around me. Shine Your light through me as I walk with my hand in Yours. I give this day to You and trust that the light You give me is just the amount I need for the step I'm on.

> *This is the message which we have heard from Him and declare to you, that God is light and in Him is no darkness at all. If we say that we have fellowship with Him, and walk in darkness, we lie and do not practice the truth. But if we walk in the light as He is in the light, we have fellowship with one another, and the blood of Jesus Christ His Son cleanses us from all sin.*
>
> 1 JOHN 1:5-7 NKJV

Your Most Important Decision

*But as for me and my household,
we will serve the Lord.*

JOSHUA 24:15 NIV

Some decisions we make in life are everlasting. We see throughout history how proper and improper decisions have changed the history of mankind.

Joshua faced the same dilemma for his family as we do for our family. Which god to worship? The gods of the world or *the* God—Jehovah?

Choosing whom to worship is the most basic question of our life. Joshua was a man of courage, strength, determination, and faith. He was a leader to his family and nation. As recorded in today's Scripture reading, Joshua states that we worship the gods we want to. For Joshua and his family, they will serve the Lord.

Which of the gods will you serve? Your life today is a consequence of the decisions you made yesterday. Are you tired of being a slave to poor decisions of the past? If so, you can have the freedom and joy of being in Christ. You do not have to continue to suffer the pain of yesterday; today you can commit to turning your life around.

Paul writes in Romans 10:9-10 (NIV), "That if you confess with your mouth, 'Jesus is Lord,' and believe in your heart that God raised him from the dead, you will be saved. For it is with your heart that you believe and are justified, and it is with your mouth that you confess and are saved."

Can you make a decision today about this promise? It will be the best decision of your life. Don't delay. Don't wait until it's too late. The writer of Ecclesiastes 3:1 (NIV) states, "There is a time for everything, and a season for every activity under heaven."

Three times a soldier in a hospital picked up the hymn "Will You Go?" which was scattered as a tract. Twice he threw it down. The last time, he read it, thought about it, and, taking his pencil, wrote deliberately in the margin these words: "By the grace of God, I will try to go, John Waugh, Company G, Tenth Regiment, P.R.V.C." That night, he went to a prayer meeting, read his resolution, requested prayers for his salvation, and said, "I am not ashamed of Christ now; but I am ashamed of myself for having been so long ashamed of Him." He was killed a few months later. How timely was his resolution!

Today is the appointed time. Make that decision for the first time, or reconfirm a previous decision that you and your family will serve the Lord.

Father God, each day I must choose what god I will worship. May I, as Joshua did, choose Jehovah God. I want to serve You with all my heart and soul. Please renew that desire in me on a daily basis. I love You. Amen.

One Hundred and One Pizzas

*P*hil and I were headed out the door for a much-needed date night. The boys and the babysitter took a vote and decided pizza was their dinner choice. Before I left, I made a quick, familiar call to Papa John's.

And until that particular call, I hadn't realized how "familiar" the Rothschild–Papa John's connection had really become!

The call began with the predictable routine, "Thanks for calling Papa John's. Will this be pickup or delivery?" I proceeded to tell the perky female on the other end of the line that it would be delivery and provided her my phone number before she even had a chance to ask for it.

With great excitement, her voice exploded in my earpiece. "Ma'am, this is the hundred and first pizza you've ordered from us! Congratulations."

I was slightly less excited than she was. "Are you sure?" I asked.

She could barely contain her excitement as she scrolled through her computer and recounted when my first purchase was.

"Umm...that's a lot of pizza," I said.

My feeble math brain began to calculate what I must have spent over the last several years on tomato sauce and mozzarella cheese. "Yikes" I said, "that's a lot of dough—I mean money! Do I get anything free from you for this grand accomplishment?"

She giggled. "Just our congratulations."

After I finished the order, I hung up and got in the van with Phil. I was in shock. Who buys 101 pizzas?

Well, obviously I had, and I was embarrassed. That meant there were 101 times I had not cooked dinner, 101 times I had tossed paper plates on the table instead of setting it, and 101 times I had tipped the delivery guy much too little.

But I refuse to let this pizza milestone be bad news.

There are some positive aspects to this pizzeria connection. It also means that there were 101 occasions over the last several years where our family relaxed a little more, 101 times we lingered at the table a little longer, and 101 times we all agreed about the dinner menu.

If you look at it that way, I have nothing to be embarrassed about. On 101 occasions, I was actually promoting healthy habits in my family. Which really makes pizza the ultimate health food (or not).

So to all of you busy women who keep the pizza industry thriving, I say a hearty congratulations. Don't be ashamed or embarrassed that you're not serving a homemade meal on fine china every night. Instead, celebrate that you're serving your family a memory that makes your home a special place to be.

Find easy ways to keep family life fun.

Believe me, I can think of at least 101.

Taste and see that the Lord is good (Psalm 34:8 NIV).

Victoria's Little Secret

Like an apple tree among the trees of the
forest is my lover among the young men.

SONG OF SONGS 2:3 NIV

Victoria has a little secret and I'm not in on it! This came to me when I found a gift certificate to Victoria's shop while cleaning out my office. *Oh, her,* I thought, a little disappointed. Not that I don't like Victoria. It's just that the thought of wearing something that is scratchy, over-revealing, and undersized doesn't give me the motivation I need to make a special trip to the mall.

Upon closer investigation, I doubled over in laughter as I realized the certificate was more than ten years old! My husband, Art, found no humor in the situation and offered to use it to buy me a gift. I just smiled back at him and requested that he remember two things: warmth and comfort! Does Victoria make flannel pj's?

Whether it's because of changes in our bodies, sleep deprivation, time constraints, financial pressures, or a myriad of other things, marriage changes after kids. But it doesn't have to be for the worse. Instead of hoping things will magically reignite and get better, I've decided to actively pursue a richer relationship with my husband. It will be a matter of choice, not chance. Here are some of my newly resolved choices:

Seduce him. Oh, gasp, is that allowed to be said in a Christian book? Absolutely! I know when my husband has been left wanting for too many days in a row, he gets cranky. Think for a minute if your husband was your only source for food. But every time you went to him to get this nourishment you not only wanted but also needed, he said back to you, "Not now. I'm too tired. I have a headache." Most husbands would love it if their wives were a little more intentional about initiating intimate connections, so seduce him.

Serve him. I can feel eyes rolling on this one, but when was the last time I really looked for something Art wanted and did it for him? Sometimes the thing we least want to do in our marriage might be the very thing that could help our relationship the most. Instead of becoming offended the next time your spouse asks if you can do something for him, why not see it as an opportunity to invest in your marriage? It just might work wonders.

Simply be sweet to him. Why is it that I can be *so* kind to strangers and then—just seconds later—impatient and *unkind* to those I love most? I don't want short fuses, quick tempers, and rushed conversations to be the legacy I build with my husband. I have to make the choice to swallow my cutting remarks and simply be sweet!

So, my little hidden gift certificate actually has served me well. It was a sign that I need to make some adjustments and investments. I think I'll ask Art if I can accompany him to the mall. And no, I won't be in search of flannel. Maybe I'm starting to clue in to Victoria's little secret after all.

> *Dear Lord, help me to remember that sex within marriage is a blessing for both me and my husband. God, give us a desire for each other that will reignite the romantic spark in our relationship. Thank You, Lord, for the privilege to be a wife. In Jesus' name. Amen.*

Words of Faith When You Wonder If Life Has Any Purpose

*W*hy was I born? What is the purpose of my existence? What am I worth to God?

Have you ever asked yourself these questions? I have. In fact, I was considering all this just the other day as I sat in my big, old chair (where I often pray), worshipping our Father by rehearsing aloud all that He is and has done. As I did, my mind went to the amazing truths of Ephesians 1. I thought of the magnificence and power of our Father in creating the world and in forming man from the dust of the earth. Then I thought of Ephesians 1:4 (NASB): *"He chose us in Him before the foundation of the world"*!

Awesome, isn't it? To think that even before God created the heavens and the earth, He knew you and me, and He chose us!

Following this, my mind went to the fact that God has the course of history all planned out. God's plan wasn't broadsided by Satan in the Garden when that evil deceiver tempted Adam and Eve to sin. Everything was already in place, for Jesus was already the Lamb of God, slain before the foundation of the world. And so I began to thank our Father for making "known to us the mystery of His will," and for "the administration of the mystery…hidden in God" for all these ages (Ephesians 1:9-10; 3:9-10 NASB).

God has a plan, and neither man nor the devil can thwart it.

Then my mind went on to Ephesians 2:10 where He tells us that before the foundation of the world our Father prepared the good works that we are to walk in! Talk about understanding our worth! Talk about knowing that our lives have a purpose!

Do you know this truth, my friend? And are you living in the light of it?

Do you realize how absolutely precious you are to God? Do you realize the significance of your life? It has a purpose. A specific purpose! As Ephesians 1:11 (NASB) says, we live "according to His purpose"—and His purpose is always the very best!

You are not an accident! You are not useless. You are not worthless. You are not unredeemable. Your worth and purpose in this life do not depend on who you are, on what you have done, or on what has been done to you. Your worth and purpose do not depend on where you have been, even if you have been to the very precipice of hell.

Your worth and purpose depend on God and God alone—His will, His calling, His choosing, His love.

> *He chose us in Him before the foundation of the world, that we would be holy and blameless before Him. In love He predestined us to adoption...through Jesus Christ to Himself, according to the kind intention of His will* (Ephesians 1:4-5 NASB).

Full Power

[I pray] that you may know…his incomparably
great power for us who believe.

EPHESIANS 1:18-19 NIV

'm moving in!" I announced to the bewildered builder.
Our new house wasn't quite finished, but I was tired
of waiting. It didn't have electrical hookup yet, but I figured
if the construction workers could operate from the little bit
of electricity from a saw box attached to the power pole, I
could too.

"Okay, Mrs. Jaynes," the builder said. "You can move in,
but you can turn on only a few lights at a time. If you want
to take a hot shower, you'll have to turn everything else off
for the water to heat up. You can turn on the oven, but you
can't have anything else on at the same time. If you move into
this house, it will be like camping out in a very nice tent."

Yes! I had won! We moved in.

It was fun at first, but I quickly grew tired of cold showers
and takeout meals. And candlelight dinners soon lost their
appeal. We were thrilled when the electrician removed the
temporary box and flipped the switch to give us full power.

I turned on all the lights, fired up the oven, and took a hot shower…all at the same time.

I thought of how this situation is similar to our Christian walk. Sometimes we live off partial power spiritually. We have access to the power of God through the Holy Spirit. Why do we settle for a few volts when we could operate fully charged with all circuits wide open?

When I mentioned this to God, He reminded me that His power is always available. We just need to connect to the true Power Source every day.

A Child's Faith

A little child will lead them.

ISAIAH 11:6 NIV

"And dear God," my little boy whispered, "I pray that you give Mommy and Daddy another Jaynes baby."

After four years of praying for God to bless us with a second child, we realized that might not be His plan for our family. However, every night my little boy, Steven, prayed for another "Jaynes baby." But how do you tell someone to stop praying a prayer?

As I pondered this dilemma, God took care of it for me. Just before his fifth birthday Steven and I were sitting at his child-sized table eating peanut butter and jelly sandwiches. He looked up at me, and with all the wisdom of the prophets asked, "Mommy, have you ever thought that God might want you to have only *one* Jaynes baby?"

"Yes, son, I have," I said. "And if that's the case, I'm glad He gave me everything I ever wanted in one package when He gave me you."

"Well, what I think we ought to do is to pray until

you're too old to have one. Then we'll know that was His answer."

Steven had no idea how old "too old" was. He knew Sarah in the Bible was 90 when she delivered Isaac. But whatever the outcome, Steven wasn't having a problem with God saying no. My son knew I said no to him many times, and no didn't mean "I don't love you." Rather it meant "I'm your parent, and I know what's best for you."

God taught me a great lesson that day. Through Steven's childlike faith, God gave me an example of the attitude of trust I should have toward my heavenly Father who loves me and knows what's best for me...and sometimes that means accepting when His answer is no.

Learning to Walk

When both of my children learned to walk, they didn't get very far without falling. They fared much better if they reached up and took my hand. Or their father's hand. We were able to guide them away from danger and get them safely where they needed to go. But sometimes they quickly headed off without our help. My son would end up falling down and hurting himself, or my daughter would wander off to someplace she wasn't supposed to go and get into trouble. Occasionally we *allowed* those things to happen because we wanted them to eventually learn to walk *without* our assistance. Of course, we did step in and protect them when we saw danger. But our goal was always to prepare them for the day when they would no longer need our help. And we were thrilled when we saw them experience that joy of freedom for the first time.

Learning to walk with our heavenly Father is somewhat different. He wants us to reach up and take His hand, but He doesn't want us to *ever* let go. In fact, His desire is that we become *more* and *more* dependent upon Him for every step. That's because He wants to take us to places we've never been. To heights we can't even imagine. In order to do that, we have to go through the low valleys, treacherous mountains, rough terrain, and narrow paths of life—places where we could easily get lost or off the track. And there is definitely no way we can just head off on our own and expect to arrive safely in the place He has planned for us. And, quite opposite of the way we teach our children, we will *never* know the joy of *true* freedom until we understand we cannot take a single step without His help.

But it's up to us to take the first step. We must look into the face of God, reach up to take His hand, and say, "Lead me in the path You have for me, Lord. From this day on I want to walk with You. I take this step of faith and I trust You to meet me here. Align my heart with Yours."

Once you've taken *that* first step, God will show you other steps to take. He will teach you how to walk in the light of His truth, revelation, and love.

Prayer Light

Father God, I don't want to take one step without You. I reach up for Your hand and ask that You lead me in Your way. Thank You that no matter where I am right now, even if I have gotten way off course, in this moment as I put my hand in Yours, You will make a path from where I am to where I need to be. And You will lead me on it. I love that Your grace abounds to me in that way. And though I can't see exactly where I am going, I'm certain that *You* can and will enable me to get to where I need to be. Thank You, Lord, that You are teaching me how to walk in total dependence upon You, for I know therein lies my greatest blessing.

You will show me the path of life;
In Your presence is fullness of joy;
At Your right hand are pleasures forevermore.

PSALM 16:11 NKJV

A Yielding of the Heart

He has brought down rulers from their thrones,
and has exalted those who were humble.

LUKE 1:52 NASB

꧁

In the New Testament we find the word "humility" to
mean a personal quality of dependence on God and
respect for other people. It is not a natural human instinct
but is a God-given virtue acquired through holy living.

While the mind of the natural man is selfish and proud,
the essence of Jesus' mind is unselfish and loving toward
others. Christ was our great example of a proper walk: pleasing to God.

Our hearts must be transformed by the Holy Spirit so
that we can reflect God's love to others through the humble
example of Jesus.

Corrie ten Boom, an unbelievable Dutch woman who
survived the horror of World War II while in the confines of
the German death camps, received a lot of praise for what she
did during her confinement, and yet she remained unfazed
by all the tributes. When asked how she managed to stay
so humble among all these honors she humbly replied, "I

accept every compliment as a flower and say thank you, and each evening I put them in a bunch and lay them at Jesus' feet, where the praise belongs."

Our world is full of men and women who are eager to take God's honor and heap it on their own heads. But God has a way of humbling us. From my own experience in life I know that I need to come before His throne with open arms and humbly bow before Him, seeking whatever He has for my life. We all need to learn this lesson of humility in life, because God has promised that if we don't humble ourselves, He will do it for us.

When Christ entered into the Greek world, they hated the quality of humility, but Jesus entered as a humble Savior. He became obedient to God's will, which led to His death on the cross. Throughout Jesus' walk on this earth He taught people to be humble before God and man.

In today's passage we see that God will exalt those who are humble. Humility comes from God and results in the praise of God.

Father God, You know how I want to lay down my bouquet of flowers at Your feet and give You all the praise. I know I am nothing without You. You have taken an ordinary woman and exalted her to a point at which I don't feel adequate. Thank You for fulfilling Your promise in me. Through my life may You be richly praised and lifted up. I am humbled that You can use me in life. Let me touch people so they know they have seen and felt Jesus. Amen.

Elizabeth George

Counting on God's Grace and Peace

Grace to you and peace be multiplied.
1 Peter 1:2 NKJV

❧

*Y*ou're a special woman. I know it. Do you know how I know? You're pursuing grace and peace by spending time in these devotions and in God's Word. When God lives within us, His Spirit causes us to yearn for a gentle calm in our lives.

Are you struggling or suffering? Are you facing a painful loss? A common response women have when they're first asked to contemplate a gentle and quiet spirit is to declare, "But I can't be like that. I can't remain calm when there's trouble." True…if we're relying on our own strength. But when we appropriate God's great enablers—His grace and His peace—we can achieve gentleness and calmness even during hard times. We just need to…

- *count on God's grace.* It's given. It's here. It's available.

- *pray for God's grace.* Your awareness of God's grace will expand when you give more things and more of you to Him.
- *get on with life.* Regardless of our struggles, it's possible—and important—to have something positive to show for our suffering, including how much God loves us, cares for us, and provides for us.

From God's Word to Your Heart

It's wonderful to think about God's grace and peace. They are two of the loveliest gifts He bestows on us. The very words move our souls.

Grace is active and means "favor." So whatever your situation, whatever the occasion, you have God's favor. You have what you need to endure, cope, and have victory. Peter prays that God's grace will be with the people he's writing to... including you and me.

Peace, on the other hand, is passive and refers to rest. And so, dear one, whatever your situation, whatever the occasion or need, you have God's peace. You have God's rest *in* your suffering.

Yes, as we suffer for doing what's right and are enabled by the power of God's grace and enjoying His peace, as we put on God's gentle and quiet spirit and rely on the Lord instead of our human efforts and emotions, as we wait on Him to help us make sense of our suffering times, then indeed we have much to show in the end. Every time we endure hard times, we prove that the glory of the Lord is truly revealed in the end. As the psalmist declared, "Oh, taste and see that the Lord is good; blessed is the man [or woman] who trusts in Him!" (Psalm 34:8 NKJV).

> God, I cry out to You during this time of strife. Your grace and peace lead me to adopt a gentle and quiet spirit even now…especially now. I will trust in Your strength and not my own as I wait for Your healing and direction. Amen.

LYSA TERKEURST

My Friend the Atheist

*God did not send his Son into the
world to condemn the world, but to
save the world through him.*

JOHN 3:17 NIV

🍂

I have a dear friend who is a wonderful person and terrific mom. We enjoy watching our kids do sports together, and when there is time we work out together. We respect each other and care about one another, but we come from two totally different vantage points. I am a passionate, sold-out Christian. She is a staunch atheist.

Without much discussion on the subject, we basically agree to disagree. But there is something going on behind the scenes that is so very exciting…she is seeing Jesus in me.

Just a few days ago, we were discussing "true beauty" while sweating and straining through sit-ups. She told me her counselor had recently asked her to describe a person who exemplified true feminine beauty, and she'd quickly answered, "Deborah Norville." But after a little more thought, she gave the counselor my name.

I laughed and told her that the only picture that should

come to her head when she thought of me was a sweaty woman in workout clothes, a scraggly ponytail hairdo, and no makeup. How could that qualify as beautiful? Her answer stirred my heart. "Lysa, it's what you have on the inside that is so beautiful."

I was amazed. Not because I took the compliment for myself, but rather for my sweet Jesus. I am convinced she sees the reality of Jesus shining through my many cracks and is drawn to Him in me. Even an atheist has God's fingerprints all over her soul. Her innermost being was created by God's hand, and something inside her must recognize Him ever so slightly. So that is where I start witnessing to her. No lengthy debates. No theological discussions. No hellfire and brimstone. I simply live and love and make the reality of Jesus known through my interactions with her and others.

She will not care to meet my Jesus until she meets the reality of Jesus lived out through my life. What a challenge for all of us! Many people are turned off by Christians because they hear us say one thing but live out another. I so desperately want to live Jesus out loud. I want to tell the whole world about Him. I am convinced I will have the privilege to one day sit down over a cup of coffee and have my friend the atheist say, "I want what you have. You make me think God could possibly be real. Will you teach me?" And what a day that will be!

Dear Lord, thank You for the privilege to know You. Thank You for changing my bitterness into joy, my horrible past into a hope-filled future, and my broken dreams into fulfilled promises. Help me to reflect the reality of You in me. I want to lead many people to the glorious hope that can only be found in You. May it be so, every day of my life. In Jesus' name. Amen.

KAY ARTHUR

Words of Faith When You Feel Out of Focus

*D*eep down inside, are you dissatisfied...or even down-right miserable?

Most of the world feels that way at one time or another—even those who seem to have everything that should make them happy. Unfortunately, this also includes many Christians.

Have you ever wondered why? Especially here on the North American continent where we live in a land of plenty. No nation has greater access to Christian literature and teaching and programming than we do. And currently, at least, no other body of Christians has as much religious freedom as do the Christians in North America.

Yet for all our freedom, for all our resources, we are hurting, miserable, and relatively impotent. We are ignorant of the "power which is in us."

As I sat meditating on the first week's study in Henry Blackaby and Claude King's *Experiencing God*, the statement "The focus needs to be on *God*, not on *life*," caught my attention. Suddenly it all clicked into place: Misery comes when *we* are the focus of our lives.

Reason with me for a moment.

Where is much of the emphasis in the world today? Isn't it on "self"? That is certainly the focus in our society, with self-esteem, self-fulfillment, self-actualization.... But think about the emphasis in much of our Christian teaching, books, seminars, radio, and television. Isn't it also on *self*?

And what is this focus accomplishing? Are the majority of Christians any happier? Any more productive? Walking in greater power? Are they being used of God to impact their society? Statistics tell us *no*!

However, when God becomes the focus, rather than self, then everything takes second place to His will for our lives. In essence, nothing else really matters. He is the only One whom we have to please. He is the only One to whom we are truly and rightly answerable.

And we need not fear that such an attitude—the focus of pleasing God alone—will make us hard, unloving, or uncaring. If our center is God, then what He works out in our lives will reflect His character, His likeness.

When we are set free from the bondage of pleasing others (including self)—of currying others' favor and others' approval—then others (and self) will not be able to make us miserable or dissatisfied, for only what pleases God will please us.

The wonderful benefit of all this is that if you make the

will of God your focus day by day, if you seek to please Him alone, then you'll find yourself satisfied with life. Misery will slip away like a whipped puppy with its tail between its legs. Life will take on purpose.

JULIE CLINTON

I Have Decided

*Choose for yourselves this day
whom you will serve.*

JOSHUA 24:15 NIV

ecisions, decisions, decisions… every day is full of them. It starts as soon as we wake up. What will we wear? What will we make for breakfast, lunch, and dinner? What will we watch on television (then again, who gets time to sit down long enough for TV)? What chores will we do first…and the list goes on and on.

I believe that a full life is lived in the moment of a decision. For instance, when driving, you can decide whether to turn right or left to get to your destination. And in that moment, you either journey closer to where you want to go or you move farther away. In a more personal example, if a mother decides not to allow the rebellion of her children to dictate her self-worth and effectiveness as a mother, she chooses to take a step toward the full and abundant life God has for her. In John 10:10 (NIV), the Bible says, "The thief comes only to steal and kill and destroy; I have come that they may have life, and have it to the full." A full life is God's dream for us fulfilled in different ways for each individual.

When you decide to hold on to and live your dreams regardless of your circumstances, you're on your way to living in God's dream for you. Today, take a moment to think about each decision as a path to the full life God desires and dreams for you!

> *Dear heavenly Father, guide me in Your will for my life. Help me to seek Your face first and foremost before making any decision on my own. I know that apart from You, I can do nothing. Help me to stay on Your path for my life! I love You, Lord! Amen.*

Created for Relationships

"Let us make man in our image."

GENESIS 1:26 NIV

ou don't have to go very far in the Bible to realize that we are made for relationships with God and with significant others in our lives. In fact, Genesis 1:26 is the first reference in the Bible showing the Trinitarian nature of God Himself: "Let *us* make man in *our* image." We serve a relational God. Three distinct persons—the Father, Son, and Holy Spirit. One God.

The Scripture is clear—we were not made to be alone (Genesis 2:18). Yet so much today is ripping and tearing at our relationships and challenging our love and affection for our husbands, our children, our friends, and our coworkers. Our time with God is an increasingly precious commodity.

Created *not* to be alone—so many people lie in bed at night crying themselves to sleep, just wishing somebody would understand them. They long for someone to know them, just to be with them. But God doesn't want that for you. His dream is for you to be in vibrant, healthy, edifying, fruitful, refreshing, encouraging relationships. To know He is there for and with you.

Ask yourself today, *What challenges are keeping me from an intimate relationship with my Creator God? What is affecting the relationships with those I love?*

Don't let aloneness trump the joy of healthy relationships in your life.

> *Father, thank You for making me in Your image. Reveal the barriers holding me back from seeking You and help me to develop intimacy with You. Please give me the courage to face the things affecting my relationships with those I love the most. Amen.*

How to View the World

Once upon a futon, Connor confidently announced to me, "Mom, I want to be an astronaut."

He was five years old at the time and about to start kindergarten, so I figured he'd thought long and hard about this decision.

"So why do you want to be an astronaut, Connor?"

"Well," he observed, "astronauts get to walk on the moon and they can see the world better than anyone else."

"That's interesting," I replied. "How can you see the world so well from up there?"

"The world is easier to see," he explained, "when you're not in it."

My little space traveler made a poignant observation that his earthbound mom needed to recognize. It is hard to see the world clearly when you're in the midst of its routines. When we heavenly citizens spend too much time taking in the messages of the world, we become desensitized. We recognize less and less how foreign it really is to our true culture.

Sometimes we just need to blast off, get a renewed heavenly

perspective, and look back at our planet and its ways through the lens of Scripture. Then we'll see it all more clearly.

As sojourners, our customs are not those of this world; they're kingdom customs.

When the world tells us to keep a big chip on our shoulders and make our violators pay dearly, our custom is forgiveness (Matthew 6:14; Luke 17:3-4).

When the world tells us to look out for number one and remember that charity begins at home, our custom is sacrificial compassion (Ephesians 4:32; Colossians 3:12).

When the world tells us to get all we can, to buy now and pay later, our custom is wide-open generosity (Matthew 5:41-42).

When the world tells us to "just do it," our custom is self-discipline (2 Peter 1:5-8).

When the world says you can have it your way, our custom is altruism and humility (Philippians 2:3).

When the world claims that it is the real thing, our custom is to fix our eyes on unseen realities (2 Corinthians 4:18).

When the world tells us to say, "I'm worth it," our custom is to say, "He is worthy" (Revelation 4:11).

We believers are called to be in the world, yet we are equally admonished to avoid allowing the world to squeeze us into its mold.

When we soar on the wings of truth, when we're carried by the winds of grace, then we can see our world and our role in it far more clearly.

Don't become so well-adjusted to your culture that you fit into it without even thinking. Instead, fix your attention on God. You'll be changed from the inside out. Readily recognize what he wants from you, and quickly respond to it. Unlike the culture around you, always dragging you down to its level of immaturity, God brings the best out of you, develops well-formed maturity in you (Romans 12:2 MSG).

ELIZABETH GEORGE

Defining True Wisdom

*The wisdom that is from above is first pure,
then peaceable, gentle, willing to yield, full of
mercy and good fruits, without partiality and
without hypocrisy. Now the fruit of righteousness
is sown in peace by those who make peace.*

JAMES 3:17-18 NKJV

A life of lovely graciousness models the fruit of wisdom and its rare fragrances of humility and gentleness. We can tell a lot about a person's faith life by how well she sows wisdom and peace. The world judges beauty by external elements: the style of a woman's hair, the designer labels on her clothes, the monetary value of her house and car. But God's beauty pours forth in the form of edifying godly words of wisdom that bring blessings to its hearers.

Consider these definitions and explanations of the eight components James shares on spiritual wisdom, the kind that comes down from above.

- *Pure*—True wisdom is free from ulterior motives and self-interest.

- *Peaceable*—True wisdom accomplishes peace in

our relationships with others and with God.

- *Gentle*—True wisdom offers forgiveness and extends kindness and consideration to everyone.
- *Willing to yield*—True wisdom is marked by a willingness to listen and a sense of knowing when to yield.
- *Full of mercy*—True wisdom reaches out to help others.
- *Full of good fruits*—True wisdom bears "good fruits" of action.
- *Without partiality*—True wisdom does not waver or vacillate in indecision or play favorites in dispensing truth and holding to its standard.
- *Without hypocrisy*—True wisdom does not deal in deception, pretension, or selfishness.

From God's Word to Your Heart

How did you do with the checklist? Are these "good fruits" evident in your life? Did you find any of these marks of wisdom missing from your lips and your ways? Think a moment about your relationships and your effect on others. Are you a promoter of peace and righteousness?

May yours be a heart of wisdom! And may your words be filled with God's wisdom. And may your prayer be a humble request to never put yourself or your opinions above the needs of others. Become that sower of peace in your family. Speak words of mercy and be sincere in your forgiveness of others. You'll experience the gracious beauty of a life overflowing with true wisdom—God's wisdom.

God, when I rely on my wisdom and the influences of the world, I end up sowing discontent and jealousy. I don't want to rely on my emotions or the trends of the season. I want my life to bear the fruit of Your wisdom so I bring blessings to others and praise to Your name. Amen.

Mrs. Jaynes, You're Leading Again

*Wives, submit to your husbands
as to the Lord.*

Ephesians 5:22 niv

"Mrs. Jaynes, you're leading again," the ballroom dancing instructor said as she tapped me on the shoulder.

Why was it so difficult for me to relinquish control? Why would I not yield to Steve's gentle press or release? Why was I having so much trouble allowing him to lead?

"Your husband has the most difficult role," the instructor said. "He has to learn all the steps, and all you have to do is follow. His job is to make you look good, but you must be responsive to his cues."

Then I had an extraordinary moment with God as He reminded me of the symbiotic dance of marriage. The dance class was a microcosm of what God intended for marriage. Two people moving as one. Coming together and moving apart—ever connected. Fluid artistry of movement designed by God.

God then expanded on the lesson and showed me that He is the ultimate leader in the dance of life, and sometimes I refuse to relinquish control to Him. I refuse to yield to His gentle nudges and guiding touches. *I can do this on my own,* I boast. But then the dance becomes muddled, and I trip over my own two feet. Then there are no beautiful waltzes through my days or rhythmic cha-chas in time with God's beat of life. I stumble and fall when I take the lead.

But in the dance of days, when God guides me with His gentle hand and I relinquish control to my Leader, our feet move as one through the twists and turns, twirls and tilts. The flow is a choreographed masterpiece of movement, beauty, and grace.

Sharon Jaynes

Your Scars Are Beautiful to God

Let the redeemed of the Lord tell their story.
Psalm 107:2 tniv

🍂

It was just a few days after Easter, and I was reading about the resurrection of Jesus in the Gospel of John, chapter 20. I had read the story many times before, but this time God revealed something I'd never noticed before.

In my mind's eye I saw Mary weeping in the pre-dawn mist hovering over the garden and the tomb where Jesus' body had been laid three days earlier. I saw her running to tell the disciples of her conversation with the risen Lord. I imagined Peter and John gazing into the empty tomb.

"He's not here," John whispered as he peered inside. "His body is gone."

And later, as the disillusioned band of disciples huddled in their hiding place, I saw Jesus appear in their midst. He didn't knock. He didn't open the door. He simply appeared.

"Peace be with you," Jesus said.

Then I realized that the disciples didn't recognize Him.

He looked like Jesus, talked like Jesus, but…how could He be Jesus?

In order to convince them, Jesus made a simple gesture. He held out His arms and revealed His nail-pierced hands. He lifted up His tunic and uncovered His spear-pierced side.

It was then that they believed.

O God, I prayed, *they didn't recognize Jesus until He showed them His scars.*

Yes, My child, He seemed to say. *This is what I wanted you to see. They didn't recognize Jesus until He showed them His scars, and this is how others still recognize Him today—when men and women who have experienced the healing of past wounds are not ashamed to show their scars to a hurting world.*

Words of Obedience When You Face Trials

*H*ow often have you heard someone say, "The Lord has been so good to us," as they have shared something good that just happened to them?

I've heard it often…as a matter of fact, from my own lips. And yet, when I say or hear an expression like this, the thought often crosses my mind, "Would they…would I…have said this if something bad had happened instead?" Would we say, "Such and such happened…the Lord has been so good to me"?

Probably not.

We seem to associate blessing only with the goodness of God. However, to do so is to be ignorant of the purpose of the trials—the difficulties, hardships, and testings—that suddenly invade our lives (but do not seem to invade the lives of those we envy).

We see trials as robbers, bent on stealing our joy or our sense of God's blessing and goodness.

How earthbound we are!

How temporal our perspective!

To the child of God, even trials are cause for rejoicing!

> *Consider it all joy, my brethren, when you encounter various trials, knowing that the testing of your faith produces endurance. And let endurance have its perfect result, that you may be perfect and complete, lacking in nothing* (James 1:2-4 NASB).

When you encounter a trial, God says, you are to consider it all joy.

Why?

Because no matter what the trial is, it has a purpose; and that purpose is to make you "perfect and complete, lacking in nothing." The word for perfect is *teleios,* which means "complete" or "mature"...in essence, "Christlike."

And because trials are permitted by God, filtered into our lives through His fingers of love, for the purpose of making us like Jesus, we can know that no child of God is exempt from trials.

Those who seem so blessed of God, those whom you might have a tendency to envy, are also going to endure trials if they are genuinely His. However, their trials will not necessarily be the same as yours. In fact, they may be going through trials right now, but you just don't see them or recognize them.

Do you know why?

Because, Beloved, you are not the same as any other

person! You are uniquely you. So God has a unique, individual set of circumstances which He will use to refine and purify you so that you will come through the fire of affliction with the dross of your ungodliness consumed.

After Jesus told Peter how he was going to suffer and die, He said to him, "Follow Me!" (John 21:19 NASB). Peter, seeing his fellow disciple John, asked Jesus what was going to happen to him. Jesus replied, "What is that to you? You follow Me!" (John 21:22 NASB).

According to tradition, Peter was crucified, martyred during the reign of Nero. John was exiled to the Isle of Patmos and later returned to Ephesus, where he was reported to have died a natural death in old age. Yet John was no more blessed by our Lord than Peter. Both men were blessed, and the trials of their faith—unique as they were—were used to make each more like Jesus.

When trials come your way—as inevitably they will—do not run away; and do not be envious of others who seem more blessed of God because they are not enduring what you are experiencing. And don't make the mistake in the midst of your trial of not recognizing the goodness of God in allowing the trial. Consider it all joy!

To consider it all joy is to look past the temporal, down the long road to the eternal…to look beyond the trial to the end result, which is you, perfect and complete, lacking nothing.

Remember, only two things will matter when you see

your Lord: how Christlike you have become, and the quality of your work for Him.

Trials are blessings in disguise to get you to that point. If we believe this and act accordingly, we will say with Peter:

> *In this you greatly rejoice, even though now for a little while, if necessary, you have been distressed by various trials, so that the proof of your faith, being more precious than gold which is perishable, even though tested by fire, may be found to result in praise and glory and honor at the revelation of Jesus Christ* (1 Peter 1:6-7 NASB).

I'm Special Because

*I praise you because I am fearfully
and wonderfully made; your works are
wonderful, I know that full well.*

PSALM 139:14 NIV

❧

One evening our seven-year-old grandson, Chad, was helping me set the dinner table. Whenever the grandchildren come over, we have a tradition of honoring someone at the table with our red plate that says "You Are Special Today" (even though it isn't a birthday, anniversary, or other special occasion). It was natural for me to ask Chad, "Who should we honor today with our special plate?"

Chad said, "How about *me?*"

"Yes, Chad, you are special," I replied. "It's your day."

He was so proud as we all sat around the table and said our blessing. Then Chad said, "I think it would be very nice if everyone around the table would tell me why they think I'm special." Bob and I got a chuckle out of that, but we thought it might be a good idea, so we did it. After we were all through Chad said, "Now I want to tell you why I think I'm special. I'm special because I'm a child of God." Chad was so right on. Psalm 139:13-14 tells us that God knew us before we were born. He knit us together in our mother's womb, and we are wonderfully made.

When I was 7, 10, or even 22, I could not have told anyone why I was special. I didn't even talk, I was so shy. My alcoholic father would go into a rage, swearing and throwing things. I was afraid I'd say the wrong thing, so I didn't talk. My self-image wasn't too good. But the day came when I read Psalm 139, and my heart came alive with the realization that I, too, am special because I am a child of God. And so are you. We were uniquely made as He knit us together in our mother's womb.

Verse 16 says, "All the days [are] ordained for me." It's not by accident you are reading this devotion today. Perhaps you, too, need to know how very special you are. We have all been given unique qualities, talents, and gifts. And you, my dear one, have been made by God. You are His child. He loves you more than any earthly father could possibly love you. Because He is your heavenly Father, Almighty God, He cares for you even when you don't care for yourself. You are His child even when you feel far from Him. It's never your heavenly Father who moves away from you. It's you who move away from Him.

Today is ordained by God for you to draw near to Him and allow Him to be near to you. Because today is your day, my friend, "You Are Special Today." A child of God, as Chad said.

Father God, thank You for making me so special, with a heart to love You more and more each day. Please today help me to draw near to You and to feel Your presence. Thank You for being my heavenly Father. I know that I'm never alone. You are always with me. Amen.

Burnout or Rest?

I've tried to learn what causes burnout before I smell the smoke! In the past, by the time I detected the burnout, it was like an incinerator, and I was lost in its flames. I'm finally figuring out that rest must be a discipline, and sometimes discipline is hard!

Hebrews 3:19 (NIV) says, "So we see that they [the children of Israel] were not able to enter [God's rest], because of their unbelief." God has shown me that when I can't rest (or when I'm flat-out unwilling to), I'm actually unwilling to fully trust in Him.

And that, my friend, sounds a lot like unbelief.

My burnout episodes in past days found their roots in the warped, really silly belief that I had to somehow help God accomplish His will. If I didn't strive, I foolishly reasoned, well, the almighty, omnipotent Lord of the universe wouldn't be successful.

Helping God run the universe is a lofty responsibility and a tough business. It can make a girl tired! Obviously, He can handle it Himself just fine. He doesn't need our assistance; He desires our obedience. Jesus tells us, "Take my yoke upon you and learn from me, for I am gentle and humble in heart, and you will find rest for your souls" (Matthew 11:29 NIV).

I remember reading something Chuck Swindoll wrote years ago that went like this: "The zealot declares, 'I'd rather *burn* out than *rust* out.' But really, what's the difference? Either way you're out!"

I can't really think of a place in Scripture where God calls us to burn ourselves to a crisp in His service. In fact, He calls us to rest. He calls us to discipline our souls to find rest in Him, not in our accomplishments on His behalf.

Would you drive your car if the gas tank were empty? Of course not. But how often do you keep on driving yourself even when *you* are empty? Benjamin Franklin once said, "He that can take rest is greater than he that can take cities."

Do you know why he compares the ability to rest with world domination? Because both require discipline. We must discipline ourselves to rest—emotionally, mentally, and physically. (And remember, Jennifer is preaching to herself here!)

To really rest means we submit our control to God's calendar, surrender our plans to His direction, and yield our time to His schedule. Even God made time in His busy creation project to rest! So for you to do the same is to follow His example. Disciplining yourself to rest is an act of good stewardship.

The discipline of rest brings freedom that doesn't exist in the ashes of burnout. When we allow ourselves to burn out, we are rendered ineffective to all the goals and tasks that were once our priorities. To discipline ourselves to rest now is far easier than to dig ourselves out of a fire pit later.

God commanded the ancient Israelites to observe the Sabbath every seven days. And He even instructed them to give their land a rest every seven years. My friend, if the dirt needs a rest so it can continue to be fruitful, so do you!

He said to them, "Come with me by yourselves to a quiet place and get some rest" (Mark 6:31 NIV).

Julie Clinton

A Willing Heart

Trust in the Lord with all your heart and
lean not on your own understanding;
in all your ways acknowledge him, and
he will make your paths straight.

Proverbs 3:5-6 niv

As we watch others soar through life seemingly unfazed by troubles and sorrows, we may begin to think, *God may have had a dream for me too, but I missed it.* Or *I'm too far along in life for God to be able to use me now.* Or *God might want to use me, but my life is just way too messed up right now.*

Regardless of your circumstances, your background, your finances, or your skills, God is looking for a willing heart. With a willing heart you will be open to God working through you and in you. Circumstances don't matter. The condition of your heart does. Is it open? Is it ready? Is it available?

A willing heart is something you can develop. The Word says that when you draw near to God, He will draw near to you (James 4:8). God is ready and waiting whenever you are. Trust Him through everything you are going through. The secret to living God's dream for you includes having a willing heart!

Open my heart, Lord. Make it willing to yield to You and to the wonderful plans You have for my life. I am trusting that You have dreams for me far beyond what I have in mind. Amen.

Julie Clinton

An Unchanging Love

*Jesus Christ is the same yesterday
and today and forever.*

Hebrews 13:8 niv

Unemployment, illness, loss, relocation…in the midst of life's most difficult changes, you can find comfort by knowing that one thing never changes: God's love for you. He's with you in every circumstance, every life change, every situation. In fact, He's not just *with* you—He's *in* you.

Isn't that a relief? God loves you, period. You don't have to earn His love. You don't have to be worthy of it. And nothing you do or have done will keep God from loving you. What a relief to know that your failings won't keep you from the love of Christ. Nothing you can do will change His feelings for you. That's grace!

He is a God of love. His love never changes. His blessings for you abound. His favor endures from one generation to the next. His dreams for you continue to shine and hold fast through every change of your life.

Dear Lord, hold fast to me through the inevitable changes of life, both good and bad. Let me rest secure in the knowledge that Your love for me, my family, and my friends will endure forever. Amen.

LYSA TERKEURST

Before I Fly
Off the Handle Again

*Only be careful, and watch yourselves closely
so that you do not forget the things your
eyes have seen or let them slip from your
heart as long as you live. Teach them to your
children and to their children after them.*

DEUTERONOMY 4:9 NIV

It was a simple request. I had asked my daughters to practice their piano pieces before the teacher arrived for lessons. When they didn't listen to my request, I became angry.

Anger was not the correct response. The way I should have responded was to calmly reprimand their disobedience and give them a consequence for their poor choice. But anger pushed my emotions beyond calm into chaos. My voice went higher in pitch and stronger in volume. Children not practicing their piano lessons should not have caused me to get so angry. What was the real issue here?

The week before, the piano teacher had informed me

that it was evident my kids had not had enough practice time. When she said this, my mind kicked into overdrive as I defined what she must have meant by this statement. *Good moms make sure their children practice at least 30 minutes a day. Good moms help their kids stay on top of their theory assignments. Good moms ensure each child makes progress that week.*

I held these unspoken but assumed interpretations up against my reality. The reality was I had no idea if my kids had even sat at the piano once that week. When I held my reality up against what I assumed to be her standard, I fell horribly short. I let my kids' poor choices be a defining reflection of what kind of mother I am. Ever been there?

There are three fundamental parenting truths that we would do well to remember in situations like this. First, refuse to dive below the surface of people's comments and blow them out of proportion. We moms can really do a number on ourselves with crazy assumptions, misinterpretations, and dangerous comparisons. The reality was, the teacher made a simple statement that my kids could use some more practice. So, tackle that issue plain and simple.

Second, there should be consequences for irresponsibility so that the pressure to remember is on them, not me. My kids are old enough to remember to practice the piano on their own. If they make an irresponsible choice, they should feel embarrassed, not me.

And finally, I must operate in truth when it comes to my identity. Just because someone forgets to practice their piano, or does one of the hundreds of other irresponsible things kids do, does not change my identity. I am not a perfect mom, but I am a good mom. And a good mom's job is to love her kids, correct them, and model godly attitudes, actions, and reactions.

> *Dear Lord, give me Your definition of what a good mom is for my specific children. You have entrusted these precious souls to me, and I don't want to mess up. Help me hold on to Your truths and resist Satan's pull toward comparisons and assumptions. Help me keep my emotions in check and my heart in tune with You. In Jesus' name. Amen.*

Refusing to Be Afraid of the Dark

When I gave birth to my first baby, the doctor told me, "You have a boy." I didn't forget that information and have to keep asking him over and over "What was my baby?" I did not wake up in the hospital the next morning and say to the nurse, "Tell me again what I had." The minute I heard I had a son, no one had to tell me again. From that moment, I knew. An entire vision for my child's future was in place the second I was told the truth.

This experience is the same for every mother and every father. Or anyone who receives life-changing good news. God wants you to have that same certainty about Him. He wants you to be so convinced of His presence in your life that even when you can't feel it, sense it, or see it, you know He is there. He wants you to be completely sure that the light of His Spirit in you will never be put out. You don't have to keep looking for it. You don't have to doubt it. No circumstance can dim it. It is there for now and all eternity.

One of the ways God makes us certain of His light is by

allowing us to test it in the darkness. But this darkness is not to be dreaded. It is the darkness God has created for His purposes. "I form the light and create darkness…" (Isaiah 45:7 NIV). God sometimes allows things to get very dark in our lives in order to grow us up and teach us about Himself. And some things that we accomplish in darkness cannot happen in any other setting.

Think about what it's like when the power goes out in your home at night. You can barely function in the dark. You walk carefully, one step at a time, reaching out for familiar things to steady and guide you until you can find a flashlight, candle, or generator switch. If someone is holding a source of light, you reach out and take their hand so you can move together. You don't take a step until you're certain that both of you are going in the same direction.

That's exactly how God uses darkness in our lives. We're in the dark until we see *His* light in it. He wants us to reach out for *Him* so we can walk together in the same direction. He desires that we draw close so that we sense His presence at all times.

Prayer Light

Lord, thank You that because I walk with You I don't have to fear the dark. Even in the blackest night, You are there. In the darkest times, You have treasures for me. No matter what I am going through, Your presence and grace are my comfort and my light. Your Word says, "…if one walks in the night, he stumbles, because the light is not in him" (John 11:9-10 NKJV). But I know Your light *is* in me. I believe in You and know that You have lifted me out of the darkness of hopelessness, futility, and fear. I refuse to be afraid. I give my hand to You, Lord. Take hold of it and lead me. Thank You that as I take each step, the light You give me will be all I need.

> *Who walks in darkness and has no light?*
> *Let him trust in the name of the LORD*
> *And rely upon his God.*
> ISAIAH 50:10 (NKJV)

Petals

An antique Mason jar tucked away in my jewelry chest contains some of my most precious possessions.

To a casual observer, it may appear that the jar is full of mismatched potpourri. But in reality, each dried flower petal has been placed in the jar quite intentionally over the past 20 years.

Within the antique blue glass are the petals from the first roses that Phil gave me on Valentine's Day when we were dating. Mixed in with these are rose petals from my bridal bouquet, from the roses he gave me on our first wedding anniversary, and from the dozen roses that proudly graced the hospital room after the birth of our first son.

Over the years, more petals have been added. If you look through the hazy glass, you can see miniature buds that once adorned the corsage I wore on Mother's Day after our second son was born. The tiny blossom reminders of my grandmother's funeral are scattered within the potpourri, along with faded blossoms from roses that my sons presented to me at one of my speaking events.

Though each rose petal is different in color, texture, and

size, what they all have in common is that they once complemented beautiful roses, and each represents something very dear to me.

There is another Rose, a precious Rose, that is not contained in my old Mason jar. It is a Rose that first sprang up in ancient Bethlehem. It blossomed in a humble manger, in the garden of poor, ordinary, faithful parents, beneath the pure light of a bright star.

The beauty of the Rose was first beheld by some humble shepherds and later adored by some very wise men. Both humble and high were granted access to the Rose. In the Song of Solomon, many pious Bible students through the years have seen the beauty of Jesus in the one who calls Himself the Rose of Sharon. What a lovely way to communicate who He is to each of us.

The picture of a rose shows Christ's beauty, and it also shows His desirability and accessibility to each of us. The rose is the chief of flowers for its beauty and fragrance, and our Jesus is the preeminent object of our desire. The sweetness of His fragrant life and words adds beauty to our dull and colorless world.

For Christ to be the Rose of Sharon shows that He is the Rose for all. Sharon was the ancient place where roses grew in fields, plentiful and lovely. Jesus was not a rose that sprang up in a greenhouse, reserved for the rich or elite. No, He blossomed in a humble manger, where all could see, touch, and receive Him. His gospel is for all—rich, poor, old, young, seeker, and skeptic.

The Rose of Sharon yields a transcendent perfume that calls us to breathe in His beauty. If you come to the manger to see the Rose, you will notice that it is moistened with dew—the tears of mourning that remind us that He was the Rose destined to wear thorns and to shed the beauty of His scarlet petals for you and for me.

He did, my friend. You are the reason He brought His beauty to this earth. You are the reason; it was for your sin the beautiful Rose was crushed.

You are the reason the Rose arose.

Don't hide the beauty of the Rose of Sharon in a treasure box with all your other sweet memories or keepsakes. Wear the Rose upon your heart, upon your life. So many cynical, despairing people in our unhappy world need to catch the scent of His fragrance and be drawn into His garden.

> *For you know that it was not with perishable things such as silver or gold that you were redeemed from the empty way of life handed down to you from your forefathers, but with the precious blood of Christ, a lamb without blemish or defect. He was chosen before the creation of the world, but was revealed in these last times for your sake. Through him you believe in God, who raised him from the dead and glorified him, and so your faith and hope are in God* (1 Peter 1:18-21 NIV).

Don't Let Him In

*Sin is crouching at your door; it desires
to have you, but you must master it.*

GENESIS 4:7 NIV

❦

*How did this happen? How am I going to get this man
out of my house?*

Questions raced through my mind as the vacuum cleaner salesman moved from room to room sprinkling his demonstration trash on my floor and then sucking it up with his machine. For over an hour this man informed me about the danger of dust mites and the benefits of his equipment.

"I already have a vacuum cleaner," I said.

"But not like this one, you don't!"

Finally I managed to convince this determined salesman that I wasn't interested in his vacuum cleaner. He was still talking as I shoved him out the door.

Whew! What just happened here? I whispered to God as I leaned against the closed door. *Where did I go wrong?*

You let him in, God said.

Of course. God was right. I should never have let the man enter my house. Then God reminded me that I had just witnessed an example of how to win every spiritual battle. When a tempting thought comes knocking at the door, don't answer it. When a deceptive idea rings the bell, don't let it in. Once a thought crosses the threshold of the mind, it's very difficult to get it to leave. Victory is possible, but it will save much heartache and pain if we don't allow the salesman in to sprinkle his trash in our minds to begin with.

We don't want what he's selling anyway.

SHARON JAYNES

Foot Holding

*My grace is sufficient for you, for my
power is made perfect in weakness.*

2 CORINTHIANS 12:9 NIV

Something strange was going on in my head, and the doctors couldn't figure out what it was. "You'll need an MRI," the doctor decided. "Are you claustrophobic?"

I assured him I was not.

The day of the exam, a nurse strapped me on a table, taped my head down on both sides, and pushed a button that slid me into a metal tube like a hotdog in a bun. Suddenly I couldn't breathe.

"Take me out!" I yelled.

"You're having a panic attack," she said after I slid out.

"I am not! Try it again." But each time I met the same fate.

"You'll have to come back another day," she finally said.

All my life I've conquered the impossible. And what is so hard about being in a metal tube for 45 minutes? I went home and told my friend Mary Ruth about my ordeal.

"I feel like such a weenie," I confessed.

"That's baloney," she said. "You just need a friend. We'll do this together."

The next week I went back with my secret weapon (Mary Ruth). She stood at the end of the tube, held my foot, prayed, and waved like Howdy Doody. The procedure went off without a hitch.

All my life I've struggled with wanting to be self-sufficient, but through extraordinary moments like these God reminds me, "My grace is sufficient for you, for my power is made perfect in weakness." It's okay to be weak. It's more than okay; it's His plan. When we admit that we are weak, He gives us His strength.

Many times God pumps courage into us through a friend who holds our hand. In this case He used Mary Ruth to hold my foot.

LYSA TERKEURST

No More Shame

I sought the Lord, and he answered me;
he delivered me from all my fears.
Those who look to him are radiant;
their faces are never covered with shame.

PSALM 34:4-5 NIV

J still remember the outdated furniture and stale cold-
ness of the room. Women from all walks of life were
there. Our paths had crossed at this awful place, a place
where life was exchanged for death. We would now share
an unmentionable secret.

No one let her eyes meet another's. Though medical
fluorescent lights brightly lit the room, the heavy darkness
in my soul made true vision nearly impossible. What had
brought me to this place? Certainly, I had people to blame.
There was the man who sexually abused me in childhood. I
could blame my biological father. Maybe if he had given me
the love and acceptance I so desperately longed for, I would
not have come to this place. I could blame God. Why had
a loving God let such terrible things happen to me? Tears
filled my eyes and deep sobs poured from my soul in that

cold room. I knew I could not blame anyone but myself. I'd walked into this place. I'd signed the papers. I'd allowed my baby to be aborted.

I can just imagine Satan hissing as he writes his name across the victim's heart: Shame. I have felt shame's pain—a deep, constant throbbing of regret from the past mixed with dread of the future.

Let's look at when shame made its debut. Genesis 2:25 (NIV) says, "The man and his wife were both naked, and they felt no shame." Then Satan slithered onto the scene to deceive Eve. When Eve fell into sin and took Adam with her, their reaction was to hide and cover up their mistake. That's exactly what I did for so many painful years. But keeping my secret in the darkness allowed Satan to use it against me. He is the father of darkness and the author of shame. He would constantly whisper that I was worthless, and that if anyone ever found out about my secret, they would condemn me.

But that was a lie from the pit of hell. When I finally brought my sin out into the light, God met me there with grace, forgiveness, and healing. Then He gave me the courage to let Him take my shame and use it for His good. I can say without hesitation the thing that has brought me the most healing has been to share my story with other women. Now that I have seen God touching and healing others through my testimony, the shame has gone and freedom has come.

Dear Lord, I thank You for seeing me as pure, clean, spotless, and without blemish. You alone have the power to heal those parts of me that I have buried and tried to hide for so long. May Your grace be enough for me today as I trust You to work all things for Your good. In Jesus' name. Amen.

Surrendering Your Dreams

very fall in California we would cut our rosebushes
back to nearly nothing. For about four months they
looked like pathetic little dead sticks from which nothing
could ever possibly grow again. But when spring came, they
blossomed and bloomed profusely. First they grew hundreds
of little buds. Then one by one they opened and burst into
all shades of pink, purple, yellow, burgundy, and white.
Abundant, fragrant, breathtaking, life-giving flowers that
people driving or walking by would stop to admire. That's
what God wants to do with us. He wants us to be His rose
garden. He wants us to have beauty and purpose, and to offer a lifegiving fragrance to those around us. But first comes
the pruning.

When God wants to make changes in our lives, and we're
willing to let Him, He starts by cutting away all that is un-
necessary. In this process, He strips from us everything that
could hinder our future growth, in order to prepare us to
bring forth good fruit. Our life may look barren during that
time, but God is actually freeing us from anything that does

not bring forth life. This process of surrendering all to the Lord, especially our dreams and desires, is called pruning.

My husband, who has been a successful musician for thirty years, once knew that God was asking him to lay down his music for a time. He was twenty years old and already a professional piano player and writer when the Lord made it clear to him that music was an idol in his life. He had to surrender his dream of ever playing or writing again. After two years of not doing anything in the music field—he didn't even practice the piano during that time—God gave him back the dream because it now had a different place in his heart. He surrendered his dream, and he saw it resurrected. I don't believe his success would have been as far-reaching, or have had the longevity it has had, if he hadn't surrendered his dream years ago.

God puts dreams in our hearts to give us vision and inspiration and to guide us to the right path. That's why we have to make sure the dreams we have are not from our own flesh. The only way to be sure of that is to lay all of our dreams at His feet and let them die. And we must also die to them. The ones that are not from Him will be buried forever. The ones that *are* from Him will be given new life.

Prayer Light

Lord, I release all my hopes and dreams to You this day. If there is anything that I am longing for that is not to be a part of my life, I ask You to take away the desire for it so that what should be in my life will be released to me. I realize how dangerous it is to make idols of my dreams—to try to force my life to be what I have envisioned for myself. I lift up to you all that I desire, and I declare this day that I desire You more. I want the desires of my heart to line up with the desires of Your heart. As hard as it is for me to let go of the hopes and dreams I have for my life, I lay them all at Your feet. I know that You will either bury them forever or resurrect them to life. I accept Your decision and fully submit to it. Lead me in Your path, Lord. You never said life would be easy. You said You would be with me. I now take each step with the light of Your presence as my guide.

> *Beloved, now we are children of God; and it has not yet been revealed what we shall be, but we know that when He is revealed, we shall be like Him, for we shall see Him as He is.*

> 1 JOHN 3:2 (NKJV)

Serving the Lord

> *[Jesus] entered a certain village; and a certain*
> *woman named Martha welcomed Him into*
> *her house. And she had a sister called Mary,*
> *who also sat at Jesus' feet and heard His word.*
> *But Martha was distracted with much serving,*
> *and she approached Him and said, "Lord,*
> *do You not care that my sister has left me to*
> *serve alone? Therefore tell her to help her."*
>
> Luke 10:38-40 nkjv

artha and Mary. Why do we love these two sisters so much? Because at times we identify with both of them! Many of us are women on missions, whether planning a dinner party, homeschooling our children, making carpool rounds, managing a household, organizing a ministry, or running a business. With such pressured and purposed service, it's easy to lose sight of our need for passionate worship. Yes, purpose and momentum are needed. We must be Marthas at times. But like Mary, we also need to pause during our hectic schedules and commune with the Lord.

Do you more commonly relate to Martha's request for

help? She sees her sister thoroughly enjoying the visit from Jesus while she feels compelled to make everything perfect for the gathering. Have you ever hosted a dinner and realized later that you barely took time to enjoy your guests? I think many of us have Martha tendencies, so let's embrace what Jesus offers Martha.

Acknowledgment. Jesus expresses empathy. He immediately recognizes the pressure Martha is under when He says, "You are worried and troubled about many things" (Luke 10:41 NKJV). When we are weary, Jesus sees our trials and our burdens. He knows we are frazzled or frustrated.

Truth. As compassionate as Jesus is, He also leads Martha to the truth. We are to focus on only one thing, and Mary has chosen that one thing—to focus on Jesus and serve and learn from Him (verse 42).

There is nothing more important than sitting at the feet of our Lord!

From God's Word to Your Heart

The Martha vs. Mary pull in us might always take place, but hopefully we'll learn to place our emphasis on "the one thing"…the right Person…Jesus. When we take time to worship, we discover that communion with God is the starting place of all our service for God and others.

Martha and Mary were so fortunate because they were able to be with Jesus while He was living in bodily form on this earth. They could reach out and touch Him and provide

Him with a good meal. And they could sit in His physical presence, talking, asking questions, and laughing.

Although we don't get that, we have Jesus living within us, a constant presence in our lives! What can we do? We can reach out in Jesus' name to someone in need of compassion. We can serve a meal to someone who needs hospitality. We can have ongoing dialogue with God through prayer. We are so blessed! We are in the presence of our Sustainer, and we can take the strength and compassion we draw from Him to serve Him by sharing it with those in our world.

> *Lord, I want to sit at Your feet as Your disciple and friend. I want to see You smile as I give You praise and share my day. Help me turn my heart to the one thing that matters more than all else...my time with You. Amen.*

Words of Faith When You Want to Call It Quits

Are you hanging on by your fingernails?

Too worn, too weary, too weak to cry out to God anymore?

Are you ready to give up, to stop praying, to stop believing, to walk away?

Are you ready to call it quits because, as you see it, there is no way for anything to change?

Do you think *I can't bear any more. I can't deal with the incessant pain*?

If I didn't know what I know about God, I might tell you to call it quits and to get on with your life.

But because God is who He is, because our times are in His hands, and because He's the God of all flesh and absolutely nothing is too hard for Him, I have to tell you not to give up. Don't "get on with your life." Wait, wait, I say, on the Lord.

And how do you wait on the Lord? There are two things you must do.

First, learn to sit at His feet and know Him.

When Martha complained to Jesus that her sister, Mary, wasn't in the kitchen helping her, Jesus replied:

> *"'Martha, Martha, you are worried and bothered about so many things; but only one thing is necessary, for Mary has chosen the good part, which shall not be taken away from her'"* (Luke 10:41-42 NASB).

Can't we all identify with Martha? We're always preoccupied with the present business of life. We're always in a hurry, even with God.

We don't take time to let go, to relax, to be still and know that *He is God* (Psalm 46:10).

To do so involves a choice. It means that some things will not get done, that some people may not understand. But didn't Jesus say that sitting at His feet and hearing His Word was *the one thing which was needful—the thing which could never be taken away from us* (Luke 10:42)?

In other words, because of what you learn from Him and of Him, you'll always have something to hang on to—and it won't be by your fingernails!

Second, tell God you want only what He wants—whatever that means.

While such a statement, such a release of your will, your way, may terrify you at this point, it won't if you make it a practice to do the "first" thing that I mentioned: sit at His feet and know Him.

If you will give God your reputation,

...if you will seek no agenda other than God's,

...if your goal will be the same as Paul's—that Christ be exalted in your body whether by life or by death,

...if for you to live will be Christ and to die, gain,

...if you are willing to do His will no matter the cost,

...then you will never find yourself caught in despair.

Rather, you will find yourself waiting patiently on the Lord for His direction. His life will be your life...and your life, *His!*

I Will Be with Your Mouth

*Now then go, and I, even I, will be with your
mouth, and teach you what you are to say.*

EXODUS 4:12 NASB

Because of the turmoil in my home as a child, I decided I would not speak, in fear that I would say the
wrong thing. I became quiet and would grasp my mother's
leg in order to hide from people. I didn't want to be around
people; I was afraid of my own family members and certainly
strangers.

My father had a major drinking problem that put everyone on pins and needles. Everyone watched what he or she
would say, because Daddy would get mad very easily and
make life miserable for the messenger who said the wrong
thing or in the wrong way.

I was this way until I got into high school and found
myself being liked by my fellow students. As a junior I had
the female lead in our senior play, "Best Foot Forward."
My success in this performance began to instill in me some
self-confidence.

It was also at this time that I met my Bob, who made me

feel safe to be around him and his loving family. But I was very quiet and reserved for fear that I might say the wrong thing. Bob would always say, "Emilie, speak up—you've got to tell me your thoughts on this," but I was very hesitant to express myself, fearing that I would say the wrong thing.

It wasn't until I was in my late twenties, when I signed up for a Christian women's retreat in Palm Springs, that I realized God had a speaking program for my life. Since the women of my church knew that I came from a Jewish faith, they asked me if I would give a three-minute testimony at the retreat. I felt like Moses in Exodus 4:10 (NASB): "Please, Lord, I have never been eloquent, neither recently nor in time past, nor since You have spoken to Your servant; for I am slow of speech and slow of tongue." Then the Lord said to me as to Moses: "Who do you think made your mouth? Is it not I the Lord?"

So I reluctantly said, "Yes, I'll do it." I wasn't sure what I would say or how I would say it, but I had confidence that my Lord and God would be by my side.

Our key verse for today gave me great strength. God said to Moses: "Now then go, and I, even I, will be with your mouth, and teach you what you are to say." That was over 45 years ago, and He still goes before me, giving me the words to say and teaching me from His Word.

I can honestly say that God will be with your mouth. I travel all over this continent sharing with women of all denominations the words He has given me to say. Along with the spoken word, He has also entrusted me with writing more than 70 books, with well over five million books in print.

As a little girl who was afraid to speak, I didn't have the faintest idea that God would use me to touch the lives of thousands through the spoken and written word. It only happened when God saw a willingness in my spirit to be used by Him.

My testimony was so well-received by those in the audience that I received many invitations to go to their local clubs to share my story. Of course, I had to expand it beyond the original three minutes to at least a 30-minute presentation, but God richly provided the words to say.

Am I still nervous when I get up to speak? Yes—every time. I still have to rely upon Him each time I speak to give me peace and calm before I begin. I often wonder as I look out on the faces of my audience, *Why me, Lord? There are many better speakers and writers than I am.* But He always answers back, "Now then go, and I will be with your mouth and teach you what to say."

> *Father God, I am amazed that You have been able to use me—an ordinary wife, mother, and grandmother. You continue to amaze me in how You take the ordinary and make it extraordinary. May I always be willing to share my story as long as there are people who want to hear it. The "bouquet of flowers" is laid at Your feet each night. You are to receive all the glory. Amen.*

JULIE CLINTON

He Enables Me

*So Paul and Barnabas spent considerable
time there, speaking boldly for the Lord, who
confirmed the message of his grace by enabling
them to do miraculous signs and wonders.*

ACTS 14:3 NIV

nabling has been given a bad rap. It implies a weakness or inability to handle things on our own. But to be enabled by God is completely different. We may think we are strong and capable, but we will always need God's enabling.

As a daughter of the King, you do not stand alone. You do not have to be strong in all things. His dream for you includes cooperating with Him in everything you do. He wants to enable you to do what He has called you to do. Only through His power can you fulfill His purpose and see His dream come true. Jesus said that apart from Him, we cannot bear fruit (John 15:4). But you belong to Him, and through His power and His grace you are enabled to accomplish all things.

Just as God enabled Paul and Barnabas to perform miracles

and wonders, He enables you in every way to perform and accomplish everything from your daily routine tasks to the challenges you perceive as impossible. When all you want to do is yell to God, *But I can't do it*…add one more word to that plea: *alone*. God does not expect you to do what He has called you to do all by yourself.

You *can* do it! Just don't try it on your own. Turn that plea into a prayer. God will hear you.

> *O Lord, I can't do it alone. Enable me to face the tasks You set before me and to accomplish what needs to be done. Let me feel Your strength, Your comfort, and Your support throughout my day. Amen.*

JULIE CLINTON

Waiting on the Lord

*Be still before the Lord and wait patiently for
him; do not fret when men succeed in their ways,
when they carry out their wicked schemes.*

PSALM 37:7 NIV

"But Mommy, I want it *now*," cried little Suzie as she
threw a temper tantrum in the middle of the aisle. As
they left the toy store together, Suzie's mom wondered where
she went wrong. Ever do that? Have you wondered why your
child was so impulsive and needed everything *now?*

Later that evening, Suzie's mom looked at herself in the
bathroom mirror and cried...not for her daughter, but for
the financial pressure. *God, why can't this be fixed now? I
just want not to have to worry about where our next meal will
come from!* Feeling the pressure of having no money, she
was also feeling the distance of God. And she wanted it all
fixed—today.

All too often we are no different from our kids screaming
for toys in the middle of the store. Let's face it—waiting is not
easy, especially in the "I want it now" culture we live in. But
as Charles Spurgeon said, "God is too good to be unkind.

He is too wise to be confused. If I cannot trace His hand, I can always trust His heart." When you seek His counsel and wait until you have clarity, you have the freedom to move with confidence, either toward something that's good for you or away from something that isn't.

Time is a commodity, and we as women have to make the most of it. If you wait patiently for God's plan to unfold, for His dream for you to be revealed, you can live and walk in the confidence of knowing He is with you every step of the way.

> *O Lord, help me to wait patiently for You. Quiet my urge to rush ahead of Your plans for my life. In Jesus' name I pray. Amen.*

Seeing What's Right
with This Picture

*H*ave you ever found yourself angry, upset, or devastated when things didn't turn out as you'd hoped or planned? Next time that happens, look deeply into the situation and ask God to give you a new perspective.

We can usually find another way to view our situation beyond how we initially see it. Because we walk in the light of the Lord, blessings abound for us in each moment. Sometimes, though, we have to deliberately look for them. God's light does not blind us, but we can be blind to God's light. We don't always see the *whole* truth. Sometimes we see everything *but* the truth.

My daughter, Mandy, and I have developed a plan for seeing the truth whenever something goes wrong. We look at the situation and ask, "What's *right* with this picture?" We pray for God to show us how what we think of as a negative situation is actually a positive one. We take even the smallest issue and reverse it. We examine the flip side. This process can become funny as we stretch to find every positive aspect, but it keeps us protected from the cynical, hopeless, and bitter attitudes that can creep into our personalities.

For example, Mandy had a car accident when she was 16. Fortunately, the lady who hit her apologized and admitted to the police and the insurance company that she was entirely to blame. As the cars were towed away, I asked my very shaken daughter what was right with this picture.

"Well, no one was hurt," she replied.

"Yes, that's the best thing," I said. "But there is another good thing. This accident is going to make you a better driver because now you realize that even when you're doing everything right, bad things can still happen. You'll be extra aware of other drivers and how important it is to pray for God's protection as you travel. What you have learned from this might be the very thing that saves your life some day."

This is not just positive thinking or trying to make good things happen with your thoughts. This is seeing things from God's perspective and letting Him show you the truth. That means *finding* the light in what seems to be a dark situation. It's knowing that, because you have invited God into every step of your life, you can find His light there no matter how dark it seems.

Prayer Light

Lord, I lift to You the situations of my life that concern me. I lay my worries before You and ask for Your mighty intervention to show me what's right when I can only see what's wrong. I am determined to see the good, so help me not to be blinded by my own fears, doubts, wants, and pre-conceived ideas. I ask You to reveal to me Your truth in every situation. Bless me with the ability to understand the bigger picture and to distinguish the valuable from the unimportant. When something seems to go wrong, help me not to jump to negative conclusions. Enable me to recognize the answers to my own prayers. I trust You to help me see the light in every situation.

> *I would have lost heart, unless I had believed*
> *That I would see the goodness of the Lord*
> *In the land of the living.*
> PSALM 27:13 (NKJV)

In the Midst of Mystery

stillborn baby, a fatal car wreck, a freak accident…
these are all mysteries that cause us anguish and raise
questions in our hearts. A wayward child, a terminal dis-
ease, a terrorist attack…isn't an all-powerful God supposed
to show His power by intervening in such baffling, tragic
circumstances?

When a human mystery like the Bermuda Triangle or
the disappearance of Amelia Earhart remains unsolved, we
are intrigued, but when a divine mystery takes center stage
in our lives, we can easily fall into despair.

Why? Because mysteries leave us with questions, not
answers.

Unanswered questions are the unwelcome companions
to human suffering. Rarely does an answer emerge from
suffering. The more questions we ask, the more we seem
to have.

Why won't God heal when He could? Why do the innocent suffer? How can God really be good if He allows
such evil?

When an infinite God allows unanswered questions, we as

finite humans tend to attribute His silence to one of several things—either He doesn't know, He doesn't care, or He really can't do anything about it.

When God engages in mystery with us, we will sometimes create a myth to explain His "disappointing behavior" and to help us understand. We conjure up such myths because our human logic and feelings don't measure up. In so doing, however, we set up a deceitful standard. And when God doesn't meet that standard, when He doesn't clear the arbitrary height at which we've set our bar, we assume He has failed or abandoned us.

Our myths might sound like this: "If I just have enough faith, God will heal me. After all, don't I deserve His blessing? If God is powerful enough to deliver me, then He should."

The prophet Habakkuk must have struggled with (what I am calling) the failure of God. The man had questions—deep, earnest, searching questions—about suffering and justice and evil in the world. But though he sought answers from the right source, God Himself, the answers didn't turn out the way he had probably imagined.

> *How long, O Lord, will I call for help, and You will not hear? I cry out to You, "Violence!" yet You do not save.*
>
> *Why do You make me see iniquity, and cause me to look on wickedness? Yes, destruction and violence*

are before me; strife exists and contention arises
(Habakkuk 1:2-3 NASB).

Habakkuk's three-chapter dialogue with heaven doesn't end with the neat, tidy answers the man of God had been hoping for. Instead, it ends with praise.

The prophet had been hoping that coming to God would answer all the mysteries that had been distressing him, but God left him with mysteries that were even deeper still.

Even so, he'd had an encounter with the greatness and wisdom of the living God, and that had brought him to his knees. And when he was on his knees, his world began to make sense.

The prophet's satisfaction was not in the answers he received to his questions, but rather in the *encounter with the God he had questioned.* The same is true for us. Our satisfaction and peace won't be found in having all our questions answered to our satisfaction, but rather in the encounter we have with God because of the questions. The encounter provides meaning in the mystery.

I'll be honest: I usually have more questions than answers. Yet I have peace. I live with that which I cannot understand. I daily embrace the mystery of my blindness, and in this mystery I find meaning because I find God there. As with Habakkuk, the satisfaction I experience is not in the answers I receive, but rather in spending time with my God the midst of the mystery.

Oh, my friend, I long for you to have a real, life-transforming encounter with God. May we all recognize that the "failure" we may have once assigned to God is really a failure of the myths we have unwittingly embraced. Only when we reject the myths and embrace the mystery do we begin to experience the intimacy waiting for us.

Answers never satisfy; only intimacy with God does. If you are in the midst of a painful mystery, stop seeking answers and seek God instead.

He is waiting to satisfy you with Himself.

> *Though the fig tree should not blossom, nor fruit be on the vines, the produce of the olive fail and the fields yield no food, the flock be cut off from the fold and there be no herd in the stalls, yet I will rejoice in the Lord; I will take joy in the God of my salvation. God, the Lord, is my strength; he makes my feet like the deer's; he makes me tread on my high places* (Habakkuk 3:17-19 esv).

KAY ARTHUR

Words of Faith When You're Wondering If God Is Enough

ow are you doing...really doing?

I would love to knock on your front door and have you invite me in for a cup of coffee and a chat. But since time and distance keep us from doing that, this book must be the next best thing. If we could just spend some time together, when we got past the "Hi! How are you?" I would want to know "How are you doing...really doing?"

How are you doing on the inside? Are you hurting or feeling like a failure? Are you exhausted, tired of what seems like a rat race through the same old maze of life, day in and day out? Are you fighting a battle with disappointment?... depression?...discouragement? Are you feeling unloved or unlovable?

Are you questioning God, wondering why He has allowed things to be the way they are? Maybe you can't even admit this to others for fear they won't understand. Is there anger in your heart because of excruciating pain or bitter disappointment? Because you have lost someone or because your life has not been a "normal" life? Because you have been rejected, abused, neglected, or unloved?

Does the future scare you? Are you wondering about your job? Your health? Cancer? Heart problems? Your children? Are you wondering how you are going to care for your parents? How you are going to provide for your family? What will happen in your old age?

Are you worrying? Anxious because you may lose your job…or because you can't find work? Worried about the kids? About how they will turn out? About what they are being exposed to? What they might get into? Drugs? Immorality? Suicide?

Or, maybe all is well but you want to go deeper with God. You want a greater consistency of devotion to your Lord Jesus Christ. You want your life to be different, less commercial, more centered on your Lord and eternal things. You want your life to have eternal significance; you want to be used by Him more than you have been in the past.

Whatever your situation, wherever you are, the answer is always the same: *God knows your plight, your state. He knows exactly where you are and what you are going through.*

He knows, and He wants to give you a future and a hope.

Overload

In all your ways acknowledge him, and
he will make your paths straight.

PROVERBS 3:6 NIV

Do you have the type of home where nothing seems to get done? Where each room would take a bulldozer just to clean up the mess? You rush around all day never completing any one job, or if you do complete a task, there is a little one behind you, pulling and messing everything up again! There isn't one of us who *hasn't* experienced these feelings.

When I was 20, our baby daughter Jennifer was six months old. We then took in my brother's three children and within a few months I became pregnant. That gave Bob and me five children under five years old. My life was work, work, work—and yet I never seemed to get anywhere. I was running on a treadmill that never stopped and never moved ahead. I was always tired and never seemed to get enough done, let alone get enough sleep. I was fragmented, totally confused, and stressed.

Then one day during my rushed quiet time with the Lord

I read Proverbs 3:6: "In all your ways acknowledge him, and he will make your paths straight." I fell to my knees and prayed, *Please, God, direct my path. I acknowledge You to help me, Lord. I'm going to allow You to lead me and not lead myself in my power. I want Your power and direction. Lord, I'm tired. I'm on overload with husband, home, children, and meals. I have no time left over for me or anyone else. I can't even do any of us justice. Please help me to put it all together and make it work to glorify You and Your children. Amen.*

The Lord not only heard my prayer that day, but He honored it as well. I began a program that changed my life. I committed 15 minutes (at least) per day to my quiet time with the Lord. With baby Brad in hand, I got up earlier each morning. The house was quiet, and my Lord and I talked as I read His Word and prayed.

Next I committed 15 minutes each day to the organization of our home, concentrating on things I never seemed to get done: the silverware drawer, refrigerator, hall closets, photos, bookshelves, piles of papers. I committed to this for 30 days and the pattern was set. God was directing my path. Our home changed dramatically. The cloud of homemaking stress lifted, and I had new direction. The Lord redeemed my time with Him. I had more time to plan meals, make new recipes, play with the children, take walks to the park, even catch a nap from time to time.

Looking back now as a grandparent, I can truly understand the meaning of acknowledging Him in all my ways.

It's looking to God for help and comfort in *all* the ways of our life—our families, home, finances, commitments, and careers. God gives us a promise: "I will direct your path."

Father God, sometimes I feel my life is truly on overload. There are days I am confused, frustrated, and misdirected. I come to You on my knees, seeking Your undying patience and the hope You so graciously give. I ask for Your direction in my life. Make order out of disorder. Thank You! Amen.

JULIE CLINTON

Around the Table

*Blessed is the man who will eat at
the feast in the kingdom of God.*

LUKE 14:15 NIV

ome of my fondest memories have been made around our dinner table. Discussing basketball with our son, listening to the drama of our daughter's high school class, smiling with my husband...these are the moments I cherish. And of course, we love to eat good food.

Have you ever wondered what God's dinner table looks like? Think about it. I imagine beautiful urns filled with the best flowers. Heaping bowls of the ripest and most delicious fruit ever seen. Serving dishes overflowing with any kind of food you want. The most exquisite china pattern ever designed on each and every plate! To know there is a space reserved just for me is simply breathtaking!

A parable found in Luke 14 speaks of a man who went to great lengths to prepare a dinner banquet for all of his friends. When the dinner was ready, he requested that his servant go and bring his friends to the table to eat. Devastated and angry when the servant returned with no one, this man invited anyone his servant could find—people who were poor, lonely, or homeless——to come and sit at his table to eat. "I tell you, not one of those men who were invited will get a taste of my banquet" (Luke 14:24 NIV).

God's banquet table is open to anyone who will believe, but many do not accept the invitation. Do you have a place at His table? If so, thank Him today for reserving you a seat. It will be a dinner you will not want to miss!

Dear Lord, thank You for reserving a place for me at Your table! Help me to pass along Your invitation to those I meet who don't know You. Amen.

JULIE CLINTON

The Trust Fall

Trust in him at all times, O people; pour out
your hearts to him, for God is our refuge.

PSALM 62:8 NIV

Trusting God to reveal His dream in your life and give you hope often requires an extraordinary act of willpower. It's kind of like one of those "trust falls," where you fall backward into the arms of someone you trust to catch you. You give up total control and place absolute trust in that person to catch you in that moment.

God wants to teach you the same about Him—that you're not in control. He is. He wants to show you that when He seems most absent and you're falling backward, He really is most present and there to catch you. God walks beside you even when you can't see, hear, or feel Him. He provides you with what you need to get through deep pain, unbelievable circumstances, and surreal events. In your weakness, He wants you to fall backward, into His arms. Place your trust in Him and let Him prove to you that He will not disappoint.

Lord, let my trust in You grow to the point that I can lean on You in absolute confidence even when the worst is happening in my life. Stand firm and secure behind me whenever I'm about to fall. Amen.

Daddy, Do You Love Me?

I am always with you; you hold me by my right hand. You guide me with your counsel, and afterward you will take me into glory. Whom have I in heaven but you?
And earth has nothing I desire besides you.
My flesh and my heart may fail, but God is the strength of my heart and my portion forever.

Psalm 73:23-26 niv

When I was eight years old, I remember wanting one thing more than anything else…my daddy's love. I remember standing beside his chair twirling around while my heart cried out for his attention. *Daddy, do you notice me? Daddy, am I beautiful? Daddy, am I your special little girl? Daddy, do you love me?* But my daddy never gave me those words of affirmation.

While my earthly daddy didn't notice me, my heavenly Daddy did. God promises to be a father to the fatherless and fill in the emotional gaps left behind from those who have abandoned us. Throughout my whole life, He has brought experiences my way that reveal the depth of His love for me.

Last summer I had the privilege to attend the Billy Graham crusade in New York City with Billy's daughter, Ruth. Ruth and I have been friends and prayer partners for several years. We met and instantly bonded at a women's conference. To me, she is just Ruth. My friend with whom I laugh, cry, pray, and experience life. I often forget about the celebrity status of her family.

But at the crusade there was no forgetting. Famous people were all around us as we made our way through the crowd to our reserved seats. My 11-year-old daughter, Hope, who was with me, kept exclaiming, "Mom, there is Amy Grant and Vince Gill! Mom, there are the Clintons, who used to live in the White House!"

I kept wondering, *Who am I? I don't belong here with all these famous people.* But just as the questions and doubt started to creep in, Ruth handed us badges to wear. All the famous people had them on. However, our badges had a gold star on the bottom. I quickly realized the meaning of this gold star as we walked past the famous people and sat with the Graham family. The gold star meant we were part of the family.

I sat down and wiped the tear that started to make its way down my cheek. I looked up to heaven and winked at my heavenly Daddy. His voice was so tender as He once again whispered to my heart, "Lysa, you are not the child of a broken parent who couldn't give you love. You are a child of God. Yes, Lysa, I notice you. Yes, Lysa, you are beautiful. Yes, Lysa, you are My special little girl. And yes, Lysa, I love you."

Dear Lord, help me to know, believe, and walk in that truth every day. As I think back on my childhood and the gaps my biological parents left in my heart, help me to forgive and release those into Your loving hands. As Psalm 73:26 states, be my strength and my portion today and always. In Jesus' name. Amen.

ELIZABETH GEORGE

Bloom Where You're Planted

> *I want you to know, brethren, that the things*
> *which happened to me have actually turned out*
> *for the furtherance of the gospel, so that it has*
> *become evident to the whole palace guard, and*
> *to all the rest, that my chains are in Christ.*
>
> PHILIPPIANS 1:12-13 NKJV

Do you complain about your circumstances at times? Do you wish you lived in a different state or neighborhood or had a different job? Have you lamented decisions you made or mourned trials that resulted in where you stand today? We've all done these things at one time or another. But we can follow Paul's example and choose to bloom where we're planted. He did—even when he was in prison.

Paul saw the blessings of his situation. From prison he could serve God as a witness to the Roman guards who watched over him day in and day out. He wrote letters and communicated through friends so he could be an inspiration and teacher for the churches. He was an example of boldness and faithfulness to those who feared persecution because of their faith in Christ.

My friend, are you chained to something? Or, to put it another way, what are your divinely appointed circumstances? Are you a wife, a mom, a single woman, a widow, a homemaker, an employee? Consider how your situation is a blessing, and how your circumstances can help you serve Christ and further His cause.

From God's Word to Your Heart

Where does today find you? I want to leave you with yet a few more words—powerful words—from Paul. He wrote these uplifting lines in Romans 8:28-29 (NKJV): "And we know that all things work together for good to those who love God, to those who are the called according to His purpose. For whom He foreknew, He also predestined to be conformed to the image of His Son." Knowing God and trusting in His promise to work all things together for good makes us women of hope. Our God is in control of all things—even those things that appear to be negative.

When we choose to bloom where our all-wise God plants us, we will one day be able to declare with Paul, "I want you to know, brethren, that the things which happened to me have actually turned out for the furtherance of the gospel."

> God, help me accept where I am now and see the blessings and opportunities that are right here. I trust in You for my life. May I embrace what You're doing in my life so I can share with others the wonders of Your great purposes. Amen.

The Look of Love

Do not be afraid;
you will not suffer shame...
You will forget the shame of your youth.

Isaiah 54:4 niv

Her invisible cloak of shame was so heavy it dragged on the ground behind her and weighed down her petite shoulders. Hidden beneath her chocolate eyes and beautiful smile was a secret that bore down on her heart. She tried to blink back tears, but they spilled down her peachlike cheeks.

"Gina, do you want to talk about it?" I asked.

"I'm so ashamed!" she cried. "I want to tell someone, but I'm afraid. I've never told anyone before."

For the next hour or so, Gina poured out her story of fleeing the advances of her stepfather, living on the street, and engaging in prostitution at the urging of a woman who said she cared.

"Every time I did it, a part of me died," she said. "I didn't do it for long, but I've never been able to forget the shame and how dirty I felt. Even though I'm now married, have two children, and a wonderful life, I still feel dirty. It was a long time ago, but it feels like yesterday. Nobody knows—not even my husband. He always tells me how precious I am. If he knew, it would kill him."

We talked for a long time about God's forgiveness and the clean slate He offers us at the cross. Gina knew most of that in her head, but her heart was having trouble believing it could be so easy.

After we talked I asked, "Are you glad you told me?"

"Yes. Mainly because the way you're looking at me now is not any different than the way you were looking at me before you knew."

And that's the truth of grace.

Rearview Driving

One thing I do: Forgetting what is behind and
straining toward what is ahead,
I press on toward the goal.

Philippians 3:13-14 niv

I turned the steering wheel a bit to the right, a bit to the left, and then back to the right again. *Why am I having trouble backing down this straight driveway?* I wondered. It was pouring down rain, and I couldn't lean my head out of the window to back down Brenda's steep driveway. I had no other choice but to depend on my rearview mirror, and I wasn't doing too well. Several times I veered off the driveway and left tire tracks in her soggy grass.

Why is this so hard? I moaned to no one in particular.

Then an unexpected stirring answered. *You're having trouble because cars aren't meant to be driven backward...and neither are you.*

Suddenly I saw more in my rearview mirror than the steep driveway behind me. I began to see the reason many of us have trouble driving down the road of life—we spend too much time looking in the rearview mirror and not enough time looking straight ahead.

In our spiritual journey, it is beneficial to look back to see where we've been, how far God has brought us, and what He has done in our lives. But if we drive through life spending too much time looking in the rearview mirror at past mistakes, abuses, and failures with cries of "if only," we're in for a heap of trouble.

There is a warning etched onto the glass of my side mirrors: *Objects in mirror are closer than they appear.* This could be interpreted in life as, "Focusing on the past leads to a distorted view of reality." Rearview mirrors are helpful, but if we choose to drive through life looking back instead of keeping our focus forward, we're in for a rough journey.

Words of Obedience When Life Doesn't Follow Your Plan

❦

*H*ow do you handle disappointment?

Disappointment. It's like a cloud that suddenly separates you from the warmth of the Son.

A chill overcomes you and you shudder. Drawing your arms tighter around yourself doesn't help.

You hurt. Yet it is not a physical pain.

It's hard to concentrate…hard to listen to what others are saying because all you can think of is the disappointment that has intruded into your world.

There can be all sorts of reasons for disappointments, but one thing is certain: You are disappointed because something has happened that is not in accord with your desire or not in accord with your plan.

Disappointment can come because of the behavior of someone else…because of a certain alteration in your circumstances…because your plans or desires have suddenly been thwarted…because something didn't turn out the way you hoped or expected…because something you once had is gone.

How do you handle disappointment so that you are not overwhelmed…demolished…demoralized? So that you don't give up? So that you don't walk away from life thinking, *Well, it's all over now. I'll never be the same. I'll never have what I've wanted. I've missed it. It's gone…forever, gone.*

You handle it, my friend, by understanding that *disappointment is God's appointment.*

Disappointment is a trial of your faith…a test that proves the genuineness of your relationship with your God and His Word.

Disappointment is something which, strange as it may seem, has been filtered through God's sovereign fingers of love. He has allowed disappointment to slip through His fingers into your life, which He holds in the palm of His omnipotent hand.

Disappointment is something that God has deemed necessary in order to bring you to His goal—Christlikeness and fruitfulness.

This is why God had James pen the following words:

> *Consider it all joy, my brethren, when you encounter various trials, knowing that the testing of your faith produces endurance. And let endurance have its perfect result, that you may be perfect and complete, lacking in nothing* (James 1:2-4 NASB).

To "consider it all joy" sounds a little insane, perhaps even masochistic. Why consider it all joy when you are over-whelmed with pain, captured by disappointment?

Because, my friend, your God commands it. And He commands it because your obedient response will be the making of you.

If the disappointment, the trial, were not for your benefit and His glory, He would never have allowed it to seep through His fingers into your life. Not because He desires to hurt you, make you miserable, demoralize you, ruin your life, or keep you from ever knowing happiness. Rather, it is because He wants you to have every opportunity to be Christlike and fruitful. God doesn't want you to have any regrets when you see Him face-to-face.

Disappointments are God's appointments. He allows them to seep through His fingers, for in His omniscience God knows their end result will be for our good and His glory.

JULIE CLINTON

The Hands of Jesus

Be kind and compassionate to one another.

EPHESIANS 4:32 NIV

Have you ever had a colleague offer a tissue in response to your tears? A neighbor you've never met bring dinner over when she learns your mother passed away? A friend offer to keep your young children so you can fly out to your grandma's funeral? They might not all be Christians, but they are Jesus' hands and feet in dark hours.

All too often, we're uncomfortable letting anyone know that all is not right in our world. We don't want to owe anyone, so we hesitate to accept the help that comes in response to tough times.

But Jesus reaches down from heaven through other people's hands. When we refuse their help, we may actually be refusing Him. We cry out for God's help, but when it comes in the form of another human, we are loath to accept it. For some reason we suddenly let pride stand in the way of allowing God to use other people to show us His love and compassion.

If you're in the midst of tough times right now, how can

you let others use their hands to be Jesus to you? Can you accept a meal? An offer of transportation? A willingness to run errands? By saying yes, you'll let Jesus comfort you through the people He's placed specifically and purposefully in your life. Allow Him to serve you.

> *O Lord Jesus, let me see Your face in the concerned expression of a neighbor who brings me a meal. Let me feel Your arms in the arms of others who give me hugs of reassurance. Let my heart be open to receiving Your love through the people You have put in my life. Amen.*

Does God Laugh?

Whoever would love life and see good days...
1 PETER 3:10 NIV

❦

My kids make me laugh. They are so much fun to be around. Have you ever thought about when God laughs? (See Psalm 59:8.) Or does He seem too serious to you? I think God is amused by us, just as we are amused by our children.

Laugh with God. Humor can show the joy of the Christian life. Crass, worldly humor glorifies sin, puts down others, ridicules righteousness, and hurts the spirit, but godly humor encourages people, honors the Lord, and heals the soul.

Admit it—the best source of humor starts at the tip of your nose! The ability to laugh at ourselves is a sign of maturity, of healthy self-esteem, and of having our priorities straight. Author Liz Curtis Higgs tells the true story of a woman who had been given a plant. She watered it, fed it plant food, and even set it outdoors to get sun—only to discover two years later that she had been watering a silk plant! Her family still gets a laugh out of that story today.

We've all been in high-stress situations where we turn to

the next person and sigh, "Someday we'll laugh about this."
I say, why wait? Lighten up and laugh today!

> *Dear heavenly Father, fill my life with laughter. Help me to laugh at the good times and the not-so-good times. To laugh at myself for my mistakes and for little things that bring joy. May I remember that I can always rejoice in Your salvation. Amen.*

Putting On a Heart of Patience

*Be patient, brethren, until the coming of
the Lord. See how the farmer waits for the
precious fruit of the earth, waiting patiently
for it until it receives the early and latter rain.
You also be patient. Establish your hearts,
for the coming of the Lord is at hand.*

JAMES 5:7-8 NKJV

I know there are a lot of jokes made about patience ("Patience is the ability to count to ten before blasting off!" "I need patience—and I need it *now*!"), but when you're the one who's forced to wait while you suffer—or suffer while you wait—it's no laughing matter. But, my friend, as the verse above says, we need to wait patiently on the Lord.

To illustrate his point, James presents a farmer. Even if some of us don't get closer to a farm than the produce stand at a local market, we can take a look at the many ways a farmer has to employ patience. He plants his crops…and then waits for the providence of God to provide the necessary rain. Finally the early rains of the fall and the late rains of spring come.

When we're suffering, we too are to wait patiently until the coming of the Lord. How are you at waiting? Is there something God is asking you to be patient about right now?

From God's Word to Your Heart

The hope we derive from the promise of Jesus' coming helps us to wait patiently. When He arrives, He will set everything in order. He will make things right. He will correct all abuses. He will bring deliverance from our suffering. Let the certainty of the Lord's return encourage your heart as you endure hard times, moments that seem endless, and the unknowns of tomorrow.

Where is your gaze fixed? Downward…on the suffering you must endure? Or upward…in the direction from which Jesus will come? Or do you seldom think about it? Your patience will be helped when you look forward to the promise of His return. You and I live with "what is," but we have the promise of "what is to be." And in-between is the waiting time. So you can fret, worry, and pace…or you can put on a heart of patience (Colossians 3:12 NASB). Which will it be? I pray you'll choose to do what God says! "Be still [be patient], and know that I am God [the Lord who is coming again and the Judge who is indeed standing at the door]" (Psalm 46:10 NIV).

> Lord, I'm making the decision to be still and to trust in Your promises. Today is hard, but I will wait for the rain of Your love to fall upon me. I will wait with hope for Your grace to show me the way You want me to go. Amen.

LYSA TERKEURST

I Don't Love My Husband Anymore

Marriage should be honored by all,
and the marriage bed kept pure.

HEBREWS 13:4 NIV

❦

I was saddened by what my friend was sharing. She was tired of her husband, and because she had found the man she dreamed of being with, she was leaving her spouse. I was shocked by her decision.

I had been in their wedding and heard the lifetime promises made from their hearts. I had been with them to celebrate their first anniversary. I had been with them just after the births of their first and second child. I had shared their laughter, encouraged them through their tears, and enjoyed doing life with them.

While their relationship had not been perfect, they did love each other. But something was broken in their relationship, and neither of them knew how to fix it. This brokenness led to a stale quietness that seeped into their home and made each feel lonelier and more isolated than they ever knew was possible for a couple. He had grown distant. She had grown frustrated. Life was busy and finances were stressful, and they stopped making time for the romantic conversations they used to enjoy. They used to be a team and felt they could beat anything life sent their way. Now they just fought against each other. Then she met an attentive, financially secure man who seemed to be the answer to all of her unmet longings.

She traded her life for the thrill of something new, the lure of something she perceived would be so much better.

But just two years later I ran into this friend and was stunned by her confession. With tears in her eyes she admitted that she'd discovered that fairy tales don't exist. Every relationship feels exhilarating at the beginning, but then real life happens and marriage is hard work no matter whom you are married to. When I asked her to tell me about her new husband, she smiled shyly and said, "Well, he's hairy."

What?

What did she just say? My mind was spinning. Of all the words, all the descriptions, all the romantic terms I expected her to use, "hairy" was nowhere on the list. How telling that the man who was once so irresistible that she traded everything for, had now been reduced to one word…hairy!

I'm convinced that in marriage the grass isn't greener on the other side. The grass is greener where you water and fertilize it.

Dear Lord, please help my husband and me to see our

marriage for the sacred gift that it is. May I always understand that being married was not meant to make me happy but rather holy. Being married is less about having the right partner and more about being the right partner. Shape me into the wife my husband not only needs but deserves. Help me to pause before I speak or react out of anger, frustration, or selfishness. Show me how to respect, love, and give to this man in a way that honors You and brings joy to our home. In Jesus' name. Amen.

Waiting in the Wings

*H*as it ever seemed like you are waiting in the wings for the next scene of your life to start? The stage is dark and you're expecting the lights to go up and the curtain to rise. The first act may or may not have gone smoothly, but by now you've been on an extended intermission and you're beginning to wonder if the second act will ever begin.

I've found that it's best to view these waiting times by thinking of them as times of waiting on the Lord. Try it. You'll see. It's much easier to think about waiting on God than it is to be patient with your circumstances. Waiting on the Lord gives you the sense that something is going on—only you just can't see it. You are waiting in eager anticipation of what God is going to do next.

Even though it may not seem like it, as long as you are walking with the Lord you are going from "glory to glory" and "strength to strength." You are always going somewhere in God's plan. And His purpose for you is constantly being realized. But you have to be patient and wait for Him to accomplish it His way and in His time.

I performed in live theater for years. The dialogue and

stage directions were set, so all of us in the cast would do the same thing over and over, night after night. Same costumes, same words, same props, same actions. It could have been a boring experience where we ended up just going through the motions waiting for the play to be over. But we didn't, for one good reason. The audience was different every time. We performed it for new ears and new eyes each night, and that kept the play fresh for us as well.

If you ever feel like you are just going through the motions in your own life, don't let yourself become frustrated over it. Know that God's mercies to you are new every morning, and as a result, God freshly hears your words spoken to Him as well. There is no such thing as the same old prayer. Each prayer you pray, even if it's about the same thing, has new life to it every time you pray it. Every day you have another opportunity to affect your future with the words you speak to God. Even though you may not see results as soon as you would like, much is happening in the spirit realm that you don't see. Each prayer sets something in motion.

Patience is not resignation. It's joyful anticipation of the glory that is before you. Actors use that time before the curtain goes up to get focused and prepare for what's ahead. As you wait for the next scene of your life to begin, center yourself in the Lord, tell Him you are content to wait for His perfect timing.

Prayer Light

Lord, I wait upon You this day. I put my hope in Your Word and ask that You would fill me afresh with Your Holy Spirit and wash away all anxiety or doubt. Shine Your spotlight into any dark corner of my soul that needs to be exposed. I don't want my impatience or lack of trust to stand in the way of all You desire to do in me. I realize that even when my life seems to be standing still, as long as I cling to You I am moving forward on the path You have for me. As I wait on You, help me to grow in my understanding of Your ways, and not succumb to impatience or discouragement because my timetable does not coincide with Yours. Strengthen my faith to depend on Your perfect timing for my life. Help me to rest in You and be content with the step I'm on and the light You have given me.

> *...those who wait on the Lord*
> *Shall renew their strength;*
> *They shall mount up with wings like eagles,*
> *They shall run and not be weary,*
> *They shall walk and not faint.*
>
> ISAIAH 40:31 (NKJV)

JENNIFER ROTHSCHILD

A Prayer for All Seasons

Let the words of my mouth
and the meditation of my heart
Be acceptable in Your sight, O Lord,
my strength and my Redeemer.

PSALM 19:14 NKJV

How I love that verse!

It's one of my favorites, not only because I can still hear my grandmother quote it but also because I pray it all the time, and I have for years. The verse is so incredibly practical because it gives both the *standard* for our talk (acceptable in Your sight) and the *source* for our talk (my strength and Redeemer).

Our standard for the words we speak both out loud and to ourselves is not merely what is acceptable to us, but rather what is acceptable to God. In our own sight, our self talk may appear fine. But imagine the God of the universe, or Jesus, His Son, sitting in your living room and listening to you talk to yourself. Imagine Him in the passenger seat as you drive alone and talk to yourself. Imagine Him in your bathroom as you look in the mirror and say the same old destructive things to yourself.

Simply put, imagine that He is standing at the door of your thought closet, hearing each phrase of self talk that comes in. Imagine that everything you say to yourself is spoken in His sight. Would you still say the same things to yourself? Would you speak in the same way to yourself if you knew He was listening?

By the way, God *does* listen to your words and your thoughts. Every one of them.

Psalm 94:9 (NIV) asks: "Does he who implanted the ear not hear?" And the psalmist confirms, "Evening, morning and noon…he hears my voice" (55:17 NIV).

He hears what no one else does. And He cares about what you say to yourself because He cares about *you*. He is your Father, the one who made you. To insult yourself is to insult Him. If you knew for certain that He was standing beside you through the hours of your day (and He is), you would most likely hold your thoughts captive at the door of your thought closet! I would never call myself an insulting name if I could see God standing right next to me, gazing attentively. I can just imagine Him saying, "Oh, Jennifer… What did you say? That's not right. I don't make idiots. Jesus died so you would know who you are and live like it. My daughter, you are not an idiot."

Seeing God in the middle of our thought closets gives us a standard to meet with our own soul talk. But in our weakness, we often need a little help choosing and controlling our soul talk. God is not only the standard of our healthy soul talk; He can also be the source of it.

The psalmist called God his strength and his Redeemer. In other words, God was the source from whom the psalmist could draw wise words and thoughts. God's strength is our source when we are weak.

To keep vigilant control over our thoughts is difficult, isn't it? We are weak, and we need strength. My grandmother used to say (and perhaps yours did too), "If you can't say something nice, don't say anything at all!" That was usually referring to me ranting about someone or something I didn't like. But her grandmotherly admonishment applies wisely to our soul talk.

God can strengthen us to keep a guard over our lips. If we can't say anything wise, productive, or edifying, God can strengthen us to say nothing at all! When you feel weak, draw from the source—His strength.

Let me challenge you to memorize Psalm 19:14 if you haven't already. Meditate on it during the day. It will become like wallpaper in your thought closet! It will constantly keep the standard and source of wise soul talk in the front of your mind.

I leave you with a little conversation between the Lord and the prophet Jeremiah, whose belittling self talk had convinced him that he was too inexperienced, ineffective, and immature to be of any use to God. But the Lord took issue with those negative, self-defeating words of the prophet.

And the rest is history!

> *The word of the Lord came to him… "Before I formed you in the womb I knew you, before you were born I set you apart; I appointed you as a prophet to the nations." "Ah, Sovereign Lord," I said, "I do not know how to speak; I am only a child." But the Lord said to me, "Do not say, 'I am only a child.' You must go to everyone I send you to and say whatever I command you. Do not be afraid of them, for I am with you and will rescue you," declares the Lord* (Jeremiah 1:2,5-8 NIV).

His Outstretched Hand

*He was despised and rejected by men, a man
of sorrows, and familiar with suffering.*

ISAIAH 53:3 NIV

Rejection can hurt so bad that you think you want to
die. We all have experienced it from time to time,
probably from someone we cared about very deeply—a parent, husband, child, friend, brother or sister, or possibly all
the above.

What great pain this can cause, and yet we can overcome
the pain of rejection. Yes, there is life after rejection.

Jesus Himself experienced rejection. If anyone knows this
pain, it's Jesus. His own people who He came to save and
teach were the very ones who nailed Him to the cross: "He
came to that which was his own, but his own did not receive
him" (John 1:11 NIV).

My Jewish family wanted me to marry within my own
faith. Yet when I was 16, my Bob introduced me to Christ.
Within a few months Bob and I were engaged, and eight
months later we were married. My very own family, those I

loved, rejected me for my stand with Jesus and my stand to marry the Christian young man I loved.

God honored my heart and my faithfulness to Him. My family grew to adore my Bob as I do, and our family was restored.

It didn't happen all at once, but in His time, one by one, hearts were softened and attitudes changed. The pain in my heart was great, but little by little His mighty strength took over and peace filled my heart. I hung in and loved my family when it was difficult to love the attitudes and mockery thrown at me. I'm grateful today I trusted Jesus.

Isaiah prophesied that Messiah would be despised and rejected of men, yet this foreknowledge did not make the experience any less painful for Jesus. And to make it even worse, Jesus felt rejected by His own Father. When Jesus bore the sins of the world He felt deep, deep pain. He cried out, "My God, my God, why have you forsaken me?" (Matthew 27:46 NIV).

Yet in the middle of all this rejection, Jesus never abandoned the mission that God had given to Him. He never fought back against the ones who rejected Him. How did He respond? With love—love even for those who crucified Him.

Do you think the Lord knows how you feel? You bet! And the Lord Jesus offers you His strength. The Bible says that He sympathizes with our weakness and He offers His grace for our time of need. When Jesus suffered on the cross, He bore our penalty for us. He paid the price for our sins. Then He gave us a promise: "Never will I leave you; never will I forsake you" (Hebrews 13:5 NIV). No matter what happens, God will never reject you. You will never be alone again. You may be rejected by others, but remember God Almighty will always be there to comfort you. His hand is stretched out to you. All you need to do is place your hands in His. Allow His strength to empower you today.

Father God, You know rejection far better than I do. I ask You to touch me when I'm rejected (or when I feel rejected) and ease that pain. Please make me sensitive to the times when I reject people. You know that I don't want to hurt others' feelings. Protect my words, body language, and attitude, that they may heal and not reject. Amen.

His Banner over Me

*When the Holy Spirit controls our lives he
will produce this kind of fruit in us: love,
joy, peace, patience, kindness, goodness,
faithfulness, gentleness, and self-control.*

Galatians 5:22-23 tlb

I had just settled into my seat when I noticed a nice-
looking young woman boarding the plane. She was
tall and slender with a pleasant smile. Wearing jeans and a
casual top, nothing particularly made this girl stand out until
she got close enough for me to notice the pageant banner
draped across her shoulder. "Miss USA" it read in sparkly
letters.

My first thought was, *How cool...a real Miss USA.* Visions
of me and my sisters as little girls glued to the television
danced through my mind. We would all pick a favorite, root
for her the whole pageant through, and giggle and prance
about as if we were being crowned.

As others noticed Miss USA's banner, they started asking
her questions and congratulating her. The flight attendant
even made an announcement that a celebrity passenger had

just joined us. As she told everyone about Miss USA, the other passengers clapped and cheered for her. She took it all in stride and even seemed a bit bashful about the attention. That impressed me more than her title. A gentle, humble spirit in the face of such notoriety is something to be admired.

After all the fuss over Miss USA settled down, I started thinking about the banners we all wear every day. While they may not drape across our chest and be printed in bold letters that sparkle, we all say something about who we are just in our countenance and interactions with others. Galatians 5:22-23 describes for us what our banner should read: love, joy, peace, patience, kindness, goodness, gentleness, faithfulness, and self-control. The Bible calls these fruits of the Spirit, which means they're evidence to others that we are a Christian. While others may not applaud us as a celebrity, they will notice the difference it makes to have God's Spirit in us if these fruits characterize our interactions with them.

It's important to understand that exemplifying these fruits is a choice we must make every day. Just as Miss USA must intentionally put on her banner, so must we. We must make the choice moment by moment, interaction by interaction, word by word, step-by-step, day by day. When I let another driver over into my lane in traffic, when I smile and thank the grocery store clerk, when I let someone go ahead of me in the coffeehouse line, when I give a gracious answer to someone being harsh with me, when I hold the door for an elderly person, or when I carry the groceries of an overwhelmed mom to her car, I am intentionally choosing to exemplify Christ.

While the world may never applaud or crown me with glory, I imagine Jesus beaming and maybe even applauding.

> *Dear Lord, may the evidence of my love for You be the banner I put on each day. Not so that I may draw attention to myself, but rather to cause other people to want to know what makes me different. I love You, Jesus, and I want to tell the whole world about You, using words only if necessary. In Jesus' name. Amen.*

Gone with the Wind

*When Moses was forty years old, he decided
to visit his fellow Israelites...After forty
years [more] had passed, an angel appeared
to Moses in the flames of a burning bush
in the desert near Mount Sinai.*

Acts 7:23,30 niv

t was the rerelease of *Gone with the Wind.* Steven had
never seen the epic drama, so we grabbed our popcorn
and settled down to enjoy a bit of history. We watched as the
plantation owners of the Old South held grand parties and
Scarlett O'Hara batted her eyelashes at all the men crowded
around her. The scenery changed as the Civil War began, and
the Old South began to crumble. Scarlett became a widow
(twice), and Rhett Butler tried to save the day.

After about two hours, Miss Scarlett stood on a hillside
with Atlanta burning in the background and shook her fist
in the air. "As God is my witness, I will never be hungry
again," she declared.

Then the curtain fell.

Steven looked at me and said, "That was a strange way to end."

I pointed his attention back to the screen, which read: *Intermission.*

Have you ever felt like Scarlett? Your plans go up in flames, your friends desert you, and you long for the good life? I think the producers had a good idea. Maybe *we* need to take an intermission—take a deep breath, refocus on God, and remember that He's not finished with the grand drama of our lives yet.

Perhaps we're just in an intermission.

Mixed Messages

Out of the same mouth come praise and cursing.
My brothers, this should not be.

JAMES 3:10 NIV

❦

Catherine and I set out for a lazy summer stroll around the neighborhood just before dusk. When we arrived back at her house, she invited me in, and before I knew it, it was almost ten o'clock.

I called my husband, sure that he would be worried. When he didn't answer the phone, I left the following message: "Steve, I was calling to let you know I'm at Catherine's. I thought you'd be worried, but apparently you don't even care because you won't pick up the phone!" *Click.* I said my good-byes and left feeling somewhat dejected. But who should I meet along the way? My worried husband riding his bike frantically through the neighborhood searching for me. When we got back home, I quickly erased the phone message.

A few weeks later Steve called me from work.

"Sharon, have you listened to the answering machine lately?"

"No, why?"

"Well, I think there's something on there you need to hear."

I used my cell phone to call our home phone, and this is what I heard: "Hello (the voice of a sweet Southern belle), you've reached the Jaynes' residence. We're unable to answer the phone right now—(Enter the voice of Cruella De Vil)—I was calling to let you know I'm at Catherine's. I thought you'd be worried, but apparently you don't even care because you won't pick up the phone! (Return of sweet Southern belle.) At the sound of the beep, leave your number, and we'll get back with you as soon as possible." *Beep.*

The phone company explained that a lightning strike had jumbled the message.

Lord, this is so embarrassing, I prayed.

Yes, it is, He said.

Okay, Lord, I got the message.

Unfortunately, so did a lot of other people.

Giving to Others

*Do not let a widow under sixty years old be
taken into the number, and not unless she has
been the wife of one man, well reported for
good works: if she has brought up children, if
she has lodged strangers, if she has washed the
saints' feet, if she has relieved the afflicted, if
she has diligently followed every good work.*

1 TIMOTHY 5:9-10 NKJV

How can a woman know beyond a shadow of a doubt
that her life has counted? Today's lesson gives us
a checklist for godly character and a life of good works.
Let's hurry on and find out what the Lord's standards are
for those who, like you and me, yearn to lead a lovely and
useful life.

Although Paul presents the qualities of an honorable
widow, we can view his description as a model for every
woman, no matter her season or station in life. Explore the
attributes of this woman. How do you match up?

Faithful to her husband—Do you honor and respect your
husband?

Known for her good works, including parenting—If you're a mom, do you view that privileged role as a good work? It is!

Practices hospitality—Do you welcome friends and strangers into your home?

Humbly serves the saints—Do you show humility through service at home, work, church, and in your community?

Helps the afflicted—Do you lend a helping hand? Who can use your help? How about a single mom who could use an afternoon of child care? Is there someone sick or lonely who could use a visit?

Pursues every good work—Do you seek out ways to serve and follow through with good deeds?

Pursuing godliness means pursuing all of these attributes. Is such a godly goal on the top of your daily "to do" list?

From God's Word to Your Heart

I could go on and on in praise of these verses and what they've meant to me as a woman. It's what I call one of the "pink passages" of the Bible—one of the sections in God's Word that spells out for women after God's own heart exactly what it means to be a true woman of excellence. Verse 10 especially shows us God's priorities, God's standard and design for our everyday lives: "If she has brought up children, if she has lodged strangers, if she has washed the saints' feet, if she has relieved the afflicted, if she has diligently followed every good work." God calls us to a life of service.

Take a look at what you're currently doing. In what areas do you shine? In what areas could you use some improvement? Pray about both areas, dedicating yourself to God and to service in His name. There is goodness and godliness in a life of service to others.

> *Lord, I want my life to count. May my mission and vision be to serve You and others and to pursue good works with passion and sincerity. Amen.*

Words of Trust When You Are Unable to Cope

W hat are you looking for that you cannot find?

What do you need? What do you long for? What void is not being filled?

Do you think it can be met by another human being? Do you think that if you only had the right person, the right relationship, things would be different? Someone you could be secure with, someone who wouldn't fail you or abandon you, someone who would understand and always be there for you, someone who could provide for you?

If you do, you will only continue to be needy and unfulfilled.

What you need is Merry Christmas—and Happy New Year! You need the relationship that is what Christmas is all about. You need Jesus, God in the flesh, the only One who can give you access to the Father. A Father who not only promises to supply all your needs through Jesus Christ, His Son, but One who is capable and willing to do so.

My God will supply all your needs according to His riches in glory in Christ Jesus (Philippians 4:19 NASB).

But where does the "Happy New Year" come in, you might ask. Why do I follow "Merry Christmas" with "Happy New Year"?

Because that is what it can be for you if you will believe and embrace this truth in the fullest sense. Your year can and will be different. Your outlook on life can and will be radically transformed.

Oh, your circumstances may not change, the human relationships you so long to alter might remain the same, but it will be a new year for you. Why? Because you will no longer be looking to another human being to meet your needs; you will be looking to God. And God never, ever fails. He cannot fail because He is God.

He is always there. He always has the answers. Nothing can ever drive Him away. Your personality, your behavior, your response will never alter who He is or what He has promised. He is God; He cannot change.

Have you stopped to consider that everything you are going through right now—every void, every unfulfilled longing—has been permitted by a sovereign God in order to draw you to the one and only wellspring that can intimately satisfy you?

It's to draw you to God's Christmas tree—the cross—where

He hung His gift—His only begotten Son—for you. The tree where God not only displays and proves His love and commitment to you, but where you find life in death. Life through your death to all else and everyone else but Him is found at the cross.

If you are a child of God and have been miserable, dissatisfied, or unable to cope, it is because you have left the cross.

Life is there—at the cross. Nowhere else.

Peace is there—at the cross. Nowhere else.

Purpose is there—at the cross, where you find your reason for living.

If you have been miserable, dissatisfied, unable to cope, it's because you have walked away in disbelief. If you ever want your deepest needs met, you can't walk away! If you ever want to fill that void within, you can't walk away!

If your happiness is wrapped up in pleasing God—in doing His will, in serving His purposes—then no person, except you, can take your happiness away. Jesus will be your joy, and the joy of the Lord will be your strength (Nehemiah 8:10).

Stepping Out of the Past

For the first thirty years of my life, I struggled with feeling that I would never be anything more than a failure. It was not until I entirely surrendered my past to the Lord that I was able to see myself as a child of God created for *His* purposes and not a dysfunctional mistake.

The biggest problem that faced me with regard to moving out of the past was unforgiveness toward my mother for the abuse I suffered at her hands. She was mentally ill and coped with me by locking me in a closet during much of my early childhood. Even though she was verbally and physically abusive as well, the closet is what affected me the most.

When I became an adult, I was still locked in a closet emotionally. It wasn't until after I came to know the Lord and went to a Christian counselor for help with my depression that I was asked to acknowledge and confess the unforgiveness I had for my mother. As each layer of unforgiveness was stripped away, I became more and more liberated from the hurt and scars of the past.

In order to walk out of unforgiveness, we have to let go of everything except God's hand. This means releasing what needs to be released, and accepting what needs to be accepted. Even an incident that happened yesterday must be given to God so that it doesn't jeopardize our future.

If there are things in your life about which you have a choice, yet you keep making the wrong choice over and over, you are probably living in the past in some way. But when you make Jesus Lord over your past and are willing to forgive yourself and everyone else associated with it, He can set you free. That means coming to Him every time you are tempted or tormented by the problem, and asking Him to help you move forward step-by-step. When we walk with the Lord, healing, deliverance, and growth are ongoing in our lives.

One of the descriptions of light is revelation. That's where the old familiar saying "Shine a light on the situation" comes from. When you need God to shine a light on your situation, ask Him for revelation. Don't sit in the darkness of the past when God has laid out a path for you to walk in the present that is illuminated with the light of His forgiveness and revelation.

Prayer Light

Lord, I release my past to You. Everything I have done and all that was done to me I lay at Your feet. I give You my bad memories and ask that You would heal me to complete wholeness so that they no longer hurt, torment, or control me. I give You my past failures in the area of (name any reoccurring problem). Even though I may be unable to completely resist the pull of certain things on my own, I know You are able to set me free.

I confess any unforgiveness in my heart for things that have happened in the past, and I release all persons who are associated with it. I specifically forgive (name of person I need to forgive). Heal all misunderstandings or hurts that have happened between us and make things right. I know that I can never be free and healed if I tie myself to others by unforgiveness. Give me Your revelation and show me all I need to see in order to walk out of the shadow of my past and into the light You have for me today.

> *Forget the former things; do not dwell on the past*
> *See, I am doing a new thing!*
> *Now it springs up; do you not perceive it?*
> *I am making a way in the desert*
> *and streams in the wasteland.*
>
> Isaiah 43:18-19 (NIV)

Sheltering Cove

He who dwells in the shelter of the Most High
will rest in the shadow of the Almighty.
PSALM 91:1 NIV

*I*magine you are on a mini-vacation. Picture yourself sitting on a beautiful white sandy beach with the warm sun shining down on you and the crystal clear blue ocean waves lapping slowly into the small secluded cove you have discovered. You dip your toes into the sea and feel the perfect temperature of the water. All is right with the world, and you are feeling sheltered completely from the busyness and trials of life.

Now, remember that warm and fuzzy feeling and reread the key verse for today. Dwelling in the shelter of the Most High is a lot like enjoying the shelter of your little cove. At any time of the day, we have the opportunity to commune with a loving God, who can provide us with the shelter we need from anything we face. We can commune with Him through prayer and also through Bible reading. The book of Psalms is filled with "sheltering" verses!

I encourage you to rest in the shadow of your almighty

Savior. Spend time with Him, commune with Him, and allow Him to be your cove of shelter today!

Dear Lord, thank You that I can be at peace, knowing that You are my shelter. Help me to rest. Help me to make time for communion with You daily! Amen.

Picture This

> *Anyone who listens to the word but does not do*
> *what it says is like a man who looks at his face*
> *in a mirror and, after looking at himself, goes*
> *away and immediately forgets what he looks like.*
>
> JAMES 1:23-24 NIV

I love pictures! Have you ever wondered who invented the camera? Many believe George Eastman invented the roll-film camera in 1888. But actually, somebody else made the camera first. The first camera that was small and portable enough to be practical for photography was built by Johann Zahn in 1685.

Pictures allow us to capture moments in time, to make memories that last forever. And with the technology available today, we can have these keepsakes in seconds!

When it comes to memorizing Scripture, a picture captured in the mind, never to be erased, would be wonderful! James says that anyone who "looks intently into the perfect law that gives freedom, and continues to do this, not forgetting what he has heard, but doing it—he will be blessed in what he does" (James 1:25 NIV).

Do you want freedom? Do you want to be blessed? Study the Bible. Find a way to memorize Scripture and obey it. Don't just walk away from hearing God's Word at church or at a conference and forget what you learned. Write it down. Use your mind like a camera and take a "picture" of God's spoken promises that you can reflect on for years to come!

Dear Lord, help me remember Your Word. Help me learn how to memorize Scripture. I want to reflect on Your promises to me all of my life. Amen.

Thank God for Smelly Shoes

Do everything without complaining or arguing.
PHILIPPIANS 2:14 NIV

🍃

*I*n my motherhood journey, how many shoes will I pick up and put back, only to pick them up and put them back again…and again…and again?

Recently, I counted more than 14 pairs of shoes that were just within eyesight of where I was sitting. I was quite frustrated that these shoes weren't where they were supposed to be. Visions of chore charts and consequences for leaving things out started dancing about in my mind. I even went so far as to think that this was yet more evidence that my kids are not as thankful as they should be. Kids who were truly thankful for their shoes would care enough to tuck them into their closet shoe racks.

But as I mentally chided my children for their ungratefulness, I felt God gently give me a piece of my own reprimand. Was I modeling thankfulness in this moment? Scattered shoes are a normal, everyday thing with a hidden treasure about them. It's all in how I choose to look at these shoes that will determine whether I feel drained and frustrated or filled up and thankful.

I stopped and thanked God for this evidence of life. Some had grass and dirt on them as proof that our kids were healthy and strong enough to run and play. Some had scuff marks from one too many dances on the concrete outside. Some had teeth marks from our beloved dog, Champ, whose favorite pastime is chasing kids, balls, and stray shoes. One had paint on it from a school project. But all were well worn, broken in, and definitely used.

So here I am, walking life's journey in this season with soccer cleats, princess shoes, basketball high-tops, teenager-want-to-be boots, kitten bedroom slippers, and gymnastics flip-flops. Funny how these shoes tell stories of life, if only I make the choice to listen. Games won and lost, girlhood fantasies, dreams of the future, comforts of home, and expressions of style.

Maybe you've felt a little frustrated with the shoes scattered about your home as well. But the next time you pick them up, instead of letting frustration whisk you away, listen carefully to the story they tell. Listen carefully and thank God for each and every precious soul who wears those shoes.

Dear Lord, thank You for the precious people You have entrusted to me who call me Mom. It is a high honor. Please help me keep this perspective through all the ups and downs of raising children. May all of my actions and reactions reflect a gentle patience that I know is only possible in Your strength. Whether it's toys left in the den, homework papers scattered on the table, or smelly shoes by the door, help me have an attitude of thankfulness first and foremost when I see all this evidence of life. Then if You could have the Holy Spirit remind my kids to put their things where they belong every now and then, that would be great too! In Jesus' name. Amen.

Words of Grace When You're Tempted to Please Others

*W*hat will matter in eternity?

Someday soon this earthly life is all going to be over! And what will matter then?

How smart, capable, or successful we were? How loved, appreciated, or applauded we were? How much we possessed? How much we achieved? How much we accomplished?

Will it matter whether we were attractive or ugly, smart or dumb, rich or poor, known or unknown?

No!

When this earthly life is over, when all is said and done, none of these things—which now seem so important—will matter.

Only one thing will matter on "that day"—the same thing that mattered to Jesus when His 33 years on earth came to a close.

When His life on this earth was over, Jesus could honestly say,

"I glorified You on the earth, having accomplished the work which You have given Me to do" (John 17:4 NASB).

When "the day of the Lord" comes (and I think it will come sooner than we think), the only thing that will matter is that you and I have glorified Him on earth and have finished the work that He has given us to do individually.

To glorify Him means to live in such a way that our lives truly demonstrate who He is.

One of my weaknesses is seeking to please people—trying to keep everyone happy—and I have to remember that it is God whom I have to serve. He alone must be my God! If not, I'm not demonstrating who He truly is!

Am I—are we—doing what He has called us to do, to be? Or are we trying to fulfill the expectations of others?

God is our director—*and our audience. We only have to please Him.*

Jesus could say what He said in John 17:4 because He always and only pleased the Father—not Himself, not His family, not His friends, not His associates, not the crowd.

The question comes to us, then: "How am I going to know what pleases Him?"

His answer is simple…and yet not so simple.

Simple in that we'll know His will if we learn to meet with Him each day and listen to His Word.

First we must be in His book—the Bible.

Second, we must seek and ask His direction; then we must be still so that we can hear His still, small voice which tells us, "This is the way...walk in it."

Jesus' habit was to get alone with the Father. And this is where the answer to "How am I going to know what pleases Him?" is not so simple.

There's so much noise, so much pressure—there are so many people pulling on us—that being alone and quiet can be a major battle.

But the battle must be won. If it's not, then the wrong things will matter, and we won't be able to say we have glorified Him on earth and have finished the work He's given us to do. When that happens, our lives will be lived at man's direction, and we'll never satisfy our human audience.

Therefore, let's give Him thanks and do whatever is necessary to live according to His will and direction.

Nothing else really matters! We are accountable only to an audience of One.

> *Teach me Your way, O Lord; I will walk in Your truth; unite my heart to fear Your name. I will give thanks to You, O Lord my God, with all my heart, and will glorify Your name forever* (Psalm 86:11-12 NASB).

The Formula

It's a question I've been asked many times, by strangers in interviews and by friends in casual conversation. It's also a question I've been asking of myself rather often these days.

It's a question about balance. Yes, the dreaded B-word. And it usually goes something like this: "How do you find balance as a woman in ministry?" The answer is far less simple.

I've been pondering, praying, and listening to the wisdom of mentors to try to come up with an easy answer. You know, a formula. Perhaps I could discover the perfect ratio of yes and no responses to opportunities outside the home. Or maybe the quantum balance question is answered by multiplying the ages of your children to how many hours of sleep you require divided by your ideal body weight.

The answer in my case is 1.32.

Meaning…what? I should dedicate 1 hour and 32 minutes each day to (what?). Or I should eliminate 1 hour and 32 minutes of (what?) out of my schedule.

See what I mean? I've woefully decided that there is no

formula. A seasoned communicator recently told me that she simply listens to God—He tells her how often, when, and where to speak, and what and when to write.

I'm such a radical type A that I really need a little more structure from the Lord. Something I can measure my schedule and motives against. You know, a goal. I'm convinced that if I aim at nothing, I will succeed all too well at hitting exactly that. And so my pursuit brought me through the pages of Scripture and landed me at—would you believe it?—a formula.

Or is it a goal?

Whatever it is, it's found in Micah 6:8. God says (in so many words), "Here's a way to live. It's good. It's healthy. It makes sense, and it's what I want for you." He even broke it up into three parts! So for all of us type A's who don't function well in the abstract, God made it perfectly concrete.

> *He has shown you, O man, what is good;*
> *And what does the Lord require of you*
> *But to do justly,*
> *To love mercy,*
> *And to walk humbly with your God?*
> (MICAH 6:8 NKJV).

To be balanced, we need to *do justly*.

That means we implement fairness and rightness toward our family and ourselves as we fill in our empty calendar slots. Doing justly, we can say no sometimes in order to be fair to ourselves, our family, and our God. But notice the *do* in "do justly." Rather than pulling back and shrinking away from all demands, we utilize our limited time and resources in the most equitable way possible.

To be balanced, we must also *love mercy.*

This pulls our heart into the equation. Mercy mandates forgiveness and forbearance. We love mercy when we lose our stern rigidity and celebrate the fact that none of us have received what our sins really deserve. Loving mercy helps us to refuse to obsess over a perfect house, it helps us to be flexible with our time, and it allows us to shift our priorities in order to meet needs.

To be balanced, we are to *walk humbly with our God.*

This is the best part of balance, because we put ourselves in a position to intimately journey with God. Instead of trying to run ahead of Him with our agenda and commitments, we simply walk with Him, in His shadow, savoring His nearness.

Do I, Jennifer, get out of balance?

Oh yes, sometimes lurching this way and that like a washing machine with a wildly imbalanced load. But most of the time, I can tell you precisely why I am out of balance. It's that nasty, five-letter word—*pride*.

Oh, I don't mean that I become all inflated and impressed with myself. (Though I know I'm capable of that too.) No, I simply mean I'm operating with the kind of pride that has little time for God and His ways because I'm busy, spinning around in my routine. That may not look arrogant to the outsider, but it's not a picture of walking humbly.

Notice that the verse doesn't say running humbly or spinning humbly. It's simply a walk. When we keep God's pace, all will be balanced.

> *Since we live by the Spirit, let us keep in step with the Spirit* (Galatians 5:25 NIV).

Sing for Joy

Come let us sing for joy to the Lord; let us
shout aloud to the Rock of our salvation.
Let us come before him with thanksgiving
and extol him with music and song.

PSALM 95:1-2 NIV

❧

Every day is worth singing for joy. But wait...*every* day? Even *this* day?

Some days don't seem especially joyful. We all have days that we would rather never repeat again. We make a major mistake at work. A child is sick. Something is making a weird noise under the hood of the car. Our husband is crabby. No money in the checkbook. No milk in the refrigerator. All those things can steal our joy.

But the kind of joy that is easily lost and gained again when the sun shines and the paycheck is deposited, when our husband is perky and the kids are in perfect health, is not the kind of joy that the Bible talks about. The kind of joy that causes us to shout to the Lord with thanksgiving, to dance before Him, is a deeper joy that nothing in this life can steal away from us.

This joy is the joy of the Lord! The joy that comes from knowing He is the Rock of our salvation. Through Him we are washed clean from our sins and free from our past. Through Him we have the promise and the hope of eternal life and eternal joy that knows no limits. That is a joy worth singing about. That is a joy that makes every day a day for singing to the Lord!

Let my life be filled with the joy of Your salvation, Lord. When my life is empty of joy due to the problems of the world, remind me, Lord, of the great joy that only You can give. Fill me with the joy of Your salvation. Amen.

Majestic Love

How great is the love the Father has lavished on
us, that we should be called children of God!

1 JOHN 3:1 NIV

❧

*L*iving out God's dream means you know His love.
But how does that happen?

Just before my dad died, he took my hand and told me
how much he loved me. In that moment I was a little girl
all over again. Amazingly, God's love for you is greater than
what my dad communicated in that magical moment. When
you know of God's love, everything changes.

Paul wants you "to grasp how wide and long and high
and deep is the love of Christ, and to know this love that
surpasses knowledge" (Ephesians 3:18-19 NIV). God's love
reaches to every area of our lives. It's a love that never ends.
He has adopted us as daughters and has invited us to know
a love that's beyond our wildest imagination. John takes us
further and tells us to "know and rely on the love God has
for us" (1 John 4:16 NIV).

How about you? How do you experience His love?
Through the smell of fresh cut grass or the ambience of the

setting sun? Maybe you're blessed by an answered prayer, or maybe you have had to rely on Him to make a tough choice in a difficult circumstance.

Pray that God will remove any barriers that keep you from relying on His perfect, beautiful, unfailing love. Experience it to the full, and rely on it instead of your own fears. When you experience this kind of love you can truly exclaim with John, "How great is the love the Father has lavished on us!"

> *Father, thank You for loving me so lavishly. Help me to fully bask in Your love. Break down the barriers that keep me from knowing and relying on Your love for me. Amen.*

The Work of Our Hands

Confirm for us the work of our hands;
yes, confirm the work of our hands.

PSALM 90:17 NASB

F or many years I struggled with the idea of worth in my work. I didn't have an advanced college degree and I was a homemaker with five children. I was always tired, with little energy for anything else—including romancing my husband. I didn't have a good handle on who I was as a person. I found myself saying to myself:

You aren't worth much.

You don't have a career.

Your job is so mundane.

Anyone can do what you do.

You don't have enough energy to do anything else.

You're stuck in a rat race with no place to go.

Over and over these thoughts went through my head. As you can suspect, I wasn't too exciting to be around!

I'm sure many readers of today's passage feel they have little worth in their hands. They have been browbeaten into thinking that life is fleeting by and they are being left behind.

During this period in my life I was involved in a small Bible study with a few godly women who shared with us young ladies two passages of Scripture that changed my life.

One was Proverbs 31, which talked about the virtuous woman, and the other was Titus 2:4-5, which describes a wife's core role as "husband lover" and "child lover." These two sections of Scripture gave me the tools I needed to establish priorities and roles in making lifestyle decisions. I soon realized that this whole concept of work and worth was very complex and that there was no right answer to fit all situations. I realized that each woman and each family has to determine what is best for them, using biblical guidelines.

As I looked at Titus 2:4-5, I realized that God wanted me to be a lover of my husband and children. This was refreshing to me because I had looked at all these drudgeries as an end unto themselves, not as a means to fulfilling one of my primary roles as a woman. But now I found my attitude toward this work changing. I was beginning to do it out of love rather than obligation.

I also realized that I did more than fulfill this role, but the role gave me some structure and direction. Up to this point in our marriage I had been experiencing frustration and disappointment because I had no direction in marriage.

The Proverbs 31 passage also made me realize that the ideal Hebrew woman handled many activities outside the home. But even while these extra activities were going on she remained focused on her husband, children, and home.

Her husband can trust her, the passage says, because "she does him good and not evil all the days of her life" (verse 12 NASB).

With this new information, I began to shift my focus from simply doing tasks to becoming a lover of my husband and children. To this day my core focus remains in this area of my life. Even though I have gone way beyond those early beginnings, I come across countless women who don't know about or aren't willing to perform the basic focus for a married woman: being a lover of their husband and children.

When I began to change my focus, I began to realize what today's key verse, Psalm 90:17, was addressing: "Confirm for us the work of our hands; yes, confirm the work of our hands."

What's in it for me as a woman? Proverbs 31:28-29 (NASB) gives me my blessing: "Her children rise up and bless her; her husband also, and he praises her, saying: 'Many daughters have done nobly, but you excel them all.'"

When my children and husband rise up and call me blessed, then I truly know that many years ago I made the right choice when I decided to be a lover of my husband and children. Without a doubt I know that God has confirmed the work of my hands.

Father God, thank You again for sending me Titus women at a young age to help me focus my role as a wife and mother. As I stand before You today I'm assured that I made the right decision. I know that many women are confused about their role as a woman. May they somehow grasp this lifesaving concept of being a lover of their husband and children first, and then other opportunities will be opened to them. Amen.

ELIZABETH GEORGE

Living by the Holy Spirit

*And do not be drunk with wine, in which
is dissipation; but be filled with the Spirit,
speaking to one another in psalms and
hymns and spiritual songs, singing and
making melody in your heart to the Lord.*

EPHESIANS 5:18-19 NKJV

Recently I was visiting with my widowed sister-in-law. We were reminiscing through some of my brother's quips and sayings. He always had a slogan or motto for every occasion. One of them I applied just today as I wondered where to shop for a particular item. His saying guided me: "The place to go is the place you know."

In our Christian pursuits, we aren't looking for a place to shop. We're looking for ways to live Jesus. As children who walk in the light, we desire to be in the presence and under the influence of the Lord Jesus, letting His mind and His actions be ours. When we are under the influence of God's Spirit, we take on new, godly attitudes.

An attitude of joy and happiness. In the early church, Christians spoke words of encouragement through Old

Testament psalms put to music. They also sang hymns and spiritual songs of praise and personal testimony. Let's follow their lead and reveal our joy as we participate in worship.

An attitude of thankfulness. Give thanks for salvation. We need to be faithful to recall and share our before-and-after stories to inspire others. Many believers joyfully give thanks to God for the good things that happen in their lives, but Paul says we are to give thanks *always* for *all* things (Ephesians 5:20). So let's hold on to a thankful spirit when it comes to setbacks, sufferings, and disappointments.

An attitude of submission. Jesus Christ was a humble, submissive servant to the Father. We want to follow in His footsteps in every relationship.

From God's Word to Your Heart

What Christian doesn't want to please God? As Jesus said, "If you love Me, keep My commandments" (John 14:15 NKJV). How can you show your love for Christ? Paul gives you the answer in today's verses: "Be filled with the Spirit." When you choose to walk in obedience to God's Word, His Spirit will empower you to...

- give praise out of a joyful heart
- give thanks out of a grateful heart
- give honor to others out of a submissive heart

Aren't you continually in awe that the God of the universe indwells you and gives you guidance for every action when you submit your will to Him? I am! Go to the place you know—God's presence—and embrace the joy of your salvation.

> *Lord, I'm filled with awe because You are so faithful and all-powerful. Joy springs up in my heart today because I know Your commands and love. I gladly follow You with all my heart. Amen.*

Maintaining a Passion for the Present

*W*alking with God means living moment by moment with Him in the present. Some people live in the past. Some people live for the future. Others give no thought to future or past, living only for the moment. We need to find a balance.

Because our future is determined one day at a time in the present, we need to seek the leading of the Lord daily. We each have the ability to get off on our own little tangent. All it takes is a pound of presumption and a sprinkle of self-satisfaction glazed lightly with laziness, and we have the perfect recipe for missing the path.

One of the main purposes for our lives is to be extensions of God's light. He says, "Let your light so shine before men, that they may see your good works and glorify your Father in heaven" (Matthew 5:16 NKJV). When we extend the light we have been given, it brings more light to our own lives. "If you extend your soul to the hungry and satisfy the afflicted soul, then your light shall dawn in the darkness, and your darkness shall be as the noonday" (Isaiah 58:10 NKJV).

If I ever feel down and am tempted to wallow in the darkness of self-pity, I ask God to show me some way to extend His light to others. He always does. When I have shared such simple things as a phone call, a letter, a kind word, a touch, an apology, a prayer, a gift, or a helping hand, I've seen the light on my path grow brighter each time.

Just as light from the moon is a reflection of the sun, the light we give off to others is a reflection of *God's* Son. When we allow God's light to shine through us, no matter how imperfectly we feel we do that, it not only shines on those around us but it illuminates our own path as well.

So let's do that! Let's free our lights to shine now—in this hour—no matter what we feel our wattage is. Let's live in the present, believing what God says. If we need healing, let us turn to the Healer. If we need provision, let us turn to the Provider. If we need wisdom, let us ask the One who is all-wise. If we need love, let us receive God's love and pass it on to those around us. Let's not wait for *life* to be perfect before we live it. Let's not wait for *us* to be perfect before we start giving of ourselves. Let's not wait for *others* to be perfect before we start loving them. The time is now.

Prayer Light

Lord, I want to live my life the way You want me to every day. Help me not to be stuck in my past, or so geared toward the future that I miss the richness of the present. Help me to experience the wealth in each moment. I know I can only get to the future You have for me by walking one step at a time in Your will today. I realize there is no better time than the present to be Your light extended to those around me. Help me to get beyond myself and become an open vessel through which Your light can shine. Give me Your wisdom and revelation and show me all I need to see to keep me on the road You have for me. Enable me to step out of my past and keep an eye on the future by following Your light on my path today.

This is the day the Lord has made;
We will rejoice and be glad in it.
PSALM 118:24 (NKJV)

If you found these devotions meaningful, you'll enjoy reading…

Kay Arthur is a four-time Gold Medallion award-winning author and beloved international Bible teacher. Kay reaches more than 80 million people daily through radio and TV and countless more through the Internet as the featured teacher on *Precepts for Life*. She and her husband, Jack, founded Precept Ministries International in 1970. Today Precept teaches people in 150 countries and nearly 70 languages how to discover truth for themselves.

Emilie Barnes is the author of 70 books, including *The Twelve Teas® of Friendship; Cleaning Up the Clutter; Heal My Heart, Lord;* and *15 Minutes Alone with God.* She appears on over 300 radio stations as host of *Keep It Simple.* Emilie and her husband, Bob, are also the founders of More Hours in My Day time-management seminars.

ISBN 978-0-7369-0773-6 . . . . *Speak to My Heart, God*
ISBN 978-0-7369-2256-2 . . . . *Quiet Moments Alone with God*

Julie Clinton, M.Ad., M.B.A., is president of Extraordinary Women and host of EWomen conferences all across America and the author of *Extraordinary Women*. A woman of deep faith, she cares passionately about seeing women live out their dreams by finding their freedom in Christ. Julie and her husband, Tim, live in Virginia with their children, Megan and Zach.

Elizabeth George, whose books have sold more than 5 million copies, is the author of *A Woman After God's Own Heart*® (nearly 1 million copies sold) and *Walking with the Women of the Bible*. She's also a popular speaker at Christian women's events. Elizabeth and her husband, Jim, are parents and grandparents, and have been active in ministry for more than 30 years.

Sharon Jaynes is an international inspirational speaker and Bible teacher for women's conferences and events. She is also the author of several books, including *Becoming the Woman of His Dreams* and *Becoming a Woman Who Listens to God*. Sharon and her husband, Steve, have one grown son, Steven, and live in North Carolina.

ISBN 978-0-7369-2112-1 . . . . *Living God's Dream for You*
ISBN 978-0-7369-2750-5 . . . . *Windows into the Word of God*
ISBN 978-0-7369-2252-4 . . . . *Extraordinary Moments with God*

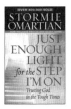

Stormie Omartian is the bestselling author of The Power of a Praying® series. She has sold over 13 million copies of her books including *The Prayer That Changes Everything*®, *The Power of a Praying*® *Woman*, *The Power of a Praying*® *Woman Bible*, and *The Power of Prayer to Change Your Marriage*. Stormie and her husband, Michael, have been married more than 35 years and are the parents of two adult children.

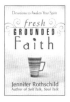

Jennifer Rothschild has been a frequent speaker on the Women of Faith tour and is the author of several books and Bible studies, including the popular *Self Talk, Soul Talk*. She has been featured on *Dr. Phil*, *Good Morning America*, and the *Billy Graham Television Special*. She is the founder of Fresh Grounded Faith conferences and of WomensMinistry.net, an online magazine for women.

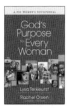

Lysa TerKeurst is a popular national conference speaker and an award-winning author of 11 books, including *What Happens When Women Say Yes to God*. She's been featured on *Focus on the Family*, *Good Morning America*, *The Oprah Show*, and in *O Magazine*. Her greatest passion is inspiring women to say yes to God and take part in the awesome adventure He has designed for them. She and her husband, Art, have five children.

ISBN 978-0-7369-2357-6 . . . . *Just Enough Light for the Step I'm On*
ISBN 978-0-7369-2575-4 . . . . *Fresh Grounded Faith*
ISBN 978-0-7369-2064-3 . . . . *God's Purpose for Every Woman*

To learn more about other Harvest House books
or to read sample chapters, log on to our website:

www.harvesthousepublishers.com

HARVEST HOUSE PUBLISHERS

EUGENE, OREGON